D0202983

On
King Lear

On *King Lear*

Kernan · Goldman · Bentley · Weiss
McFarland · Danson · Roche · Seltzer

EDITED BY LAWRENCE DANSON

Princeton University Press
Princeton, New Jersey

Copyright © 1981 by Princeton University Press

Published by Princeton University Press, Princeton, New Jersey
In the United Kingdom: Princeton University Press, Guildford, Surrey

All Rights Reserved

Library of Congress Cataloging in Publication Data will be
found on the last printed page of this book

Publication of this book has been aided by a grant from
The Whitney Darrow Publication Reserve Fund of
Princeton University Press

Clothbound editions of Princeton University Press books
are printed on acid-free paper, and binding materials are
chosen for strength and durability

Printed in the United States of America by Princeton
University Press, Princeton, New Jersey

Designed by Laury A. Egan

In Memoriam
Daniel Seltzer
1933-1980

Contents

On
King Lear

Introduction

The eight lectures gathered here were delivered at Princeton by members of the Princeton University English Department during the academic year 1978-1979. Each of the lecturers is, among other things, a Shakespearean—someone, that is, who teaches and has published scholarly criticism on the subject. (We aggrandize ourselves by counting in our number one professor emeritus, G. E. Bentley. One lecturer, the poet Theodore Weiss, is simultaneously a member of Princeton's Program in Creative Writing. This volume is dedicated to the memory of our colleague Daniel Seltzer, whose death not long after the completion of the lecture series deeply diminished us.) As noteworthy as the number is the variety, and it was this combination of circumstances—a group of professional colleagues dedicated to the same subject yet distinguished by a plurality of approaches to it—that originally made the series seem, at least as an experiment, a worthwhile undertaking.

Lecturing is less unusual for professors than listening, and one of the private benefits we intended by this series was the opportunity to listen to one another. We hoped to hear the differences in our attitudes to Shakespeare as well as the similarities, and, to bring these out better, we decided to make a single play, *King Lear*, our common ostensible focus. That there was some overlapping in the resulting lectures was a gratifying result: we exist, it turns out, within a single broad universe of discourse and we now have some assurance that the play each of us sees is, in some important particulars, the same play—not a negligible assurance in this critical age. The differences that emerged were equally reassuring; they account for some of the interest of this volume, and I will say a few words about them shortly.

First, about the present form of the lectures. Our revisions have been slight, in the hope that the book would retain some sense of the individual voice that more formal essay-writing tends to flatten. Although, as I have said, it had been our hope to listen to one another, the unavoidable distractions of academic life made it impossible for each of us to attend every lecture. When we could not hear, we nevertheless read one another's texts. So the lectures, which are presented here in the order of their delivery, occasionally contain references to lectures given subsequently—a form of prophecy known to Lear's Fool (who came before Merlin's time). In some small touches of revision, that is, we made further efforts to acknowledge what others had said, whenever in fact it had been said.

Shakespeare's variousness, nowhere more evident than in *King Lear*, licensed the lectures' variety. A pedagogical rhyme runs "age-stage-page," but it runs out long before the number of significant Shakespearean foci are in fact exhausted. The history of ideas, textual study, theater history, psychological criticism, performance theory, audience-response criticism, and "close reading" of whatever sort may all be brought to bear, but we still will not have encountered all of the Shakespearean universe. By that I mean not only the obligatory reference to Shakespeare's breadth of mind or, in Coleridge's phrase, his myriad-mindedness. I mean also to acknowledge the inevitable narrowness of even the best individual critic, and to suggest why, perhaps, eight may be better than one.

If a single theme is sounded repeatedly in these lectures, it is, I think, the sheer magnitude of *King Lear*. Daniel Seltzer, in his final lecture, gets at the size of it by way of the actor's experience of the play and the audience's experience of the actor. His lecture makes us aware of the large-scale rhythms of performance through which the play's awesome power is communicated. Michael Goldman is also concerned with the demands of the play on its actors, but his focus, complementing Seltzer's, is on characteristic details, especially in the performed sounds of the play, through which the larger structures are realized. And G. E. Bentley, seeing the stage from still a different vantage, reminds us of the facts of Shakespeare's theatrical life, his professional concerns as actor, sharer, theater owner, and poet-in-ordinary to the King's

Men—practical facts that underlie whatever magnitude the play has in performance.

Alvin B. Kernan also begins with the economic and social realities of an Elizabethan life in the theater, and progresses from these to the reconstruction of a Shakespearean pageant of history, which he finds in the plays generally and in *King Lear* specifically. Thomas McFarland is also concerned with a kind of history and politics—the timeless kind that every human being negotiates in the relations between parents and children. His emphasis on *King Lear* as a play about the family shows that its magnitude is a product also of concentration, of a paring away to reveal "the familial nucleus." My own lecture takes up the question of the play's focus in a different way, by concentrating on the peculiar difficulty of encompassing its vision of man as simultaneously vast and infinitesimal according to two different but equally valid scales of being. Theodore Weiss's reflections on the play impress us from still a different angle with the magnitude of *King Lear*, especially with the incredible, apparently intractable variety of linguistic styles and of dramatic and narrative material Shakespeare here wielded for his artistic purposes. Thomas P. Roche returns to some of the basic and inescapable questions the play poses about tragedy and tragic knowledge; his answers, from a historically grounded Christian point of view, challenge some commonly held assumptions. Roche's lecture reminds us, fittingly, that, though dramatic characters may, critics may not confidently pronounce last words.

All references to Shakespeare's works are to *The Complete Signet Classic Shakespeare*, ed. Sylvan Barnet (New York: Harcourt, Brace, Jovanovich, 1972).

Lawrence Danson

One

King Lear and the Shakespearean Pageant of History

Alvin B. Kernan

During the sixteenth and seventeenth centuries, humanist scholars and artists throughout Europe wrote histories, painted pictures, built palaces, created epic poems, and staged lavish spectacles designed to legitimize and celebrate the power of the new princes and their dynasties. In England this relationship of the humanist artist to the absolute Tudor and Stuart monarchs can be traced from the paintings of Holbein, through such works as Holinshed's *Chronicles* and *The Faerie Queene*, to the buildings of Inigo Jones, the masques of Ben Jonson, and the portraits of Van Dyck. Even though the theater for which Shakespeare wrote was a public theater, and therefore not entirely dependent on the favor of the prince, what we know of its political and social circumstances suggests that it too, like the other arts, was oriented toward the court. The chief enemies of the English public theater were the Puritan polemicists and the businessmen of the city of London, who were destined to behead a king and close the theaters, while its chief allies seem to have been the great nobles and court officials who lent their names to the acting companies, whose members would have been at the mercy of the laws against vagabonds were it not for the protection afforded by the status of being the Lord Chamberlain's Servants or the King's Men. The monarchy censored plays and licensed performances through the office of the Master of the

Revels, but it also protected the theaters, through the intervention of the Privy Council and Star Chamber, from the attempts of the city to pluck them down. The nobility supported the players by arranging and paying for performances at the various bastions of the establishment—the court, the great houses, the universities, and the inns of court.

Gerald Bentley's distinguished summary lecture shows how much more complex the social situation of the playing companies was than I have represented it, but the broad outlines are clear. Given this courtly orientation, it would be reasonable to expect that the theater would support the monarchy and its aristocratic, courtly values. And to a large extent it seems to have done so, for, as Patrick Cruttwell remarks, the theater

> sprang from, and for its appreciation demanded, a hierarchical view of society. Its tragedy is that of "noble" personalities, its comedy that of men who will not understand and remain within their social limits like Malvolio and Sir Epicure Mammon.[1]

On the surface at least, Shakespeare's plays, as Tillyard established a generation ago, dramatize the Tudor myth with its emphasis on a strong central government, the rightness of a hierarchical society reflecting in human terms a natural and supernatural cosmic scheme, the consequent dangers of disobedience and disorder, and the disasters that befall the land as a result of usurpation and the overthrow of a rightful king.

But if Shakespeare was, as I think there is little doubt, a profoundly conservative writer who became the most successful playwright of his age by teaching his audience the history of England, bringing its great heroes such as the brave Talbot and Henry V to life once again, and by serving as a political apologist for its benevolent despots, he was also, and at the same time, capable of radical, and even anarchic, conceptions of society and the powers that govern and shape it.

[1] *The Shakespearean Moment and Its Place in the Poetry of the 17th Century* (New York: Random House Modern Library, 1960), p. 151.

In other words, Shakespeare's view was neither a radical nor a conservative view of history but both at once. Something of his ambiguity toward his noble patrons and his sense of the problematical relationship of his plays to their lives and values can be glimpsed in the plays-within-the-plays, such as in *A Midsummer Night's Dream* where Theseus and the other noble members of the audience completely fail in manners and in understanding of the internal play of "Pyramus and Thisby"; or in *Hamlet* where "The Murder of Gonzago," a play dealing with matters of the most vital concern to the throne of Denmark, is performed before the royal court, only to go uncomprehended by the queen and most of the courtiers, to be interrupted and thoroughly misunderstood by the prince of the blood who has arranged for its performance, and to be, not the occasion for repentance by the murderer king, but the impetus for another dynastic murder. Whatever the effect of "The Murder of Gonzago" on the royal court of Denmark, the internal play does not in any way suggest that William Shakespeare was comfortable with the traditional view that theater made for the good health of kingdoms by revealing the past and showing great princes and their subjects the moral and historical truths of their societies.

It is, nevertheless, the frequency and ambiguity with which Shakespeare explored the social and political questions of his time that suggest most clearly how profound and how problematic was the relationship of his theater to the established political order. Nineteen of his thirty-eight plays deal directly and centrally with historical and dynastic matters. In the remaining half, primarily the comedies and romances, political questions of rule and authority are always prominent if not central: Othello is the governor of Cyprus; the question of how a state should be ruled is an important issue in *Measure for Measure*; the nature of law is basic to *The Merchant of Venice*; and a deposed duke and his tyrannous brother are key figures in even so light a comedy as *As You Like It*. Shakespeare conceived of man always in terms of his relationship to the state, and presented him as a city-dwelling animal, caught up inevitably in the historical process. Personal affairs are always intertwined with affairs of state, and only a misanthropic hermit like Timon of Athens lives unto himself without any ties to the state, and he eventually commits suicide.

Because Shakespeare was a poet, a writer of fictions, the extent to which he was also a great cultural historian is not generally recognized. He had a sharp and penetrating eye for the realistic motives and cues for passion that lie behind certain basic political stances: the unbending pride in self and the contempt for the weakness of others of a man on horseback like Coriolanus; the inability of a legitimist like Richard II to comprehend that the social order that supports him is not eternal and immutable; the political innocence of an idealistic upper-class revolutionary like Brutus; the icy efficiency of the successful prince like Octavius Caesar; and the utter cynicism about all matters of state of a hedonist like Falstaff. Shakespeare portrays with equal power certain central scenes of political life: Richard III carefully staging the occasion on which the citizens of London petition him to accept the crown; Claudius's cool and efficient management of the many tricky affairs of state in his presence chamber in the second scene of *Hamlet*; Octavius and Antony negotiating at the council table the bargain that divides the world between them; Bolingbroke's "Moscow-trial" contrivance of Richard's confession of his failures and resignation of his crown; the debate about the return of Helen to the Greeks, which resolves nothing in Priam's Trojan palace; Julius Caesar's control of his public image in the state procession at the Lupercal and before the Roman crowd shouting for him to be king.

These few examples illustrate the observant and critical eye Shakespeare had for the real attitudes and occasions that are the substance of political life, and these observations in turn rest solidly on a substratum of historical fact, although scholars have tended to ignore this aspect of his plays by treating them primarily as art with universal implications and little to do with hard facts of Elizabethan economic and social life. And indeed Shakespeare does not treat social questions in the immediate realistic terms of his great contemporary Ben Jonson, who saw the power alignments of his time, such as the connection between capitalism and protestantism, with uncanny accuracy. Rather, Shakespeare transmutes the immediate facts into poetic fables of the fall of Troy, the Wars of the Roses, and the transformation of the Roman Republic into an empire, which in turn reveal the metaphysical, moral, and psychological values brought into play and put at risk by the enormous social and economic changes of his age. But the real immediate issues of his time are there as well, woven into the story in a manner that a few examples drawn from *Lear* will suggest.

The giving away of the land, "even from this line to this, / With shadowy forests, and with champains riched, / With plenteous rivers, and wide-skirted meads" (1.1.63-65), is the beginning of the tragedy and a reflection of the central social issue of the time: the transfer of land from the old aristocracy to new entrepreneurs, and from one type of management stressing a natural relationship between estate, lord, and tenant to a new type of exploitation of the land for profit.

The old king's imaginative awareness on the heath of all the poor and homeless of the world,

> Poor naked wretches, wheresoe'er you are,
> That bide the pelting of this pitiless storm,
> How shall your houseless heads and unfed sides,
> Your looped and windowed raggedness, defend you
> From seasons such as these?
>
> (3.4.28-32)

acknowledges the "savage depression of the living standards of the lower half of the population" in Shakespeare's time, a depression created by an eight hundred percent increase in the value of land, an overall inflation rate of five hundred percent, a doubling of the population between 1530 and 1660, and a fall in real wages by half.[2]

Lear's band of followers, his hundred knights, directly re-

---

[2] Christopher Hill, *Reformation to Industrial Revolution, 1530-1780*, Pelican Economic History of Britain, vol. 2 (Harmondsworth: Penguin Books, 1969), p. 83.

flects the question of maintenance, the rights of the old feudal barons to keep private armies; and Goneril's whittling away of the knights "in the tender of a wholesome weal"—"What need one?"—reflects almost equally directly the ongoing efforts of the state to eliminate these riotous, dangerous, and uneconomic groups of armed retainers, and to change the aristocracy from a military class to dependents of the crown.

The motif of clothing, Lear's progressive stripping and reclothing, which Shakespeare thoroughly integrates into the symbolic system of *Lear*, is based on the sumptuary laws of the time, which tried to maintain class distinctions by prescribing the types of garments that men of different classes might wear.

Lear's fury when his messenger is put in the stocks and degraded is born of a sense of outrage at the violation of the traditional freedom from the law extended to the servants of a great noble. The old king's violent reaction to this indignity is no stronger than the words actually used by Sir George Grey on a similar occasion, when he insisted that a town yield up a prisoner to him: "Have him I will. . . . therefore send him me, for as I live I will try all the friends I have in England, but I will be righted. . . . If you be able to cross me in one thing I can requite your town with twenty."[3]

The close relationship between the plays and the historical events of the age is borne out not only in the single detail but in a much larger sense as well. Looking back from the present, historians see in the Tudor and Stuart age the beginnings of the change, perhaps not yet complete in our own time, that transformed the hierarchical, feudal, landed, religious, aristocratic medieval society into a democratic, capitalistic, scientific middle-class modern society. As Lawrence Stone puts it in *The Crisis of the Aristocracy*:

> Granted that change is a continuous process, that every shift has both earlier antecedents and later developments, it is nevertheless between 1560 and 1640, and more precisely between 1580 and 1620, that the real watershed

[3] Ibid., p. 52.

between medieval and modern England must be placed. It was then that the State fully established its authority, that dozens of armed retainers were replaced by a coach, two footmen, and a page-boy, that private castles gave way to private houses, and that aristocratic rebellion finally petered out; then that the north and west were brought within the national orbit and abandoned their age-old habits of personal violence; then that the British Isles, England, Wales, Scotland, and Ireland were first effectively united; then that political objectives began to be stated in terms of abstract liberty and the public interest, rather than particular liberties and ancient customs; then that radical protestantism elevated the individual conscience over the claims of traditional obedience in the family, in the Church, in the nation . . . then that capitalist ethics, population growth, and monetary inflation undermined old landlord-tenant relationships and old methods of estate management.[4]

The country and the city, the king's palace and the baronial castle, the public square and the private house, England and Britain, prince and nobles, aristocracy and the people, the individual conscience and ancient customs, nonconformity and traditional obedience to family, church, and society—these are also the major structural oppositions in the world of Shakespeare's plays. And out of these opposing facets of two world views, the medieval and the modern, emerges the Shakespearean overview or pageant of history.

Shakespeare's plays themselves tend to be less than optimistic about the possibility of men understanding much more of history than their immediate moment. Whenever Shakespeare shows one of his characters trying to understand the shape that the future will take from the present—Brutus pondering beforehand the effects of the murder of Caesar, Macbeth consulting the witches and trying to understand the future

---

[4] *The Crisis of the Aristocracy, 1558-1641*, abridged ed. (Oxford: Oxford Univ. Press, 1967), pp. 12-13.

contained in their ambiguous symbols, Henry V talking to his soldiers in the light of the campfires before Agincourt—the result is always bafflement and error. There are in Shakespeare no clear epic prospects of history like the view of the future that Michael shows Adam in books eleven and twelve of *Paradise Lost*, but there are many scenes like that which Tolstoy creates in *War and Peace* at the battle of Smolensk when Napoleon dispatches regiment after regiment into the darkness of the smoke-covered field, believing wrongly that he is controlling the outcome of the battle, while the wiser Russian marshall, Kutuzov, retires to pray. In the Shakespearean view of history, men caught in the movement of history, driven by their own passions and the historical forces at work on them, seldom can see clearly the direction their world is taking. On the rare occasions when they do understand the future, like Hector, who knows that Troy will fall if Helen is not returned, they are helpless to change the course of events, or can only respond like Henry IV to the news of another rebellion in what he at last knows to be an endless series of them initiated by his own rebellion against King Richard—"Are these things then necessities? / Then let us meet them like necessities" (*2 Henry IV*, 3.1.92-93). But most often Shakespeare's man in history is simply destroyed by forces he does not comprehend—like Cinna the poet in *Julius Caesar*, who is torn apart by the Roman mob, which confuses him with Cinna the conspirator, and then, when that mistake is cleared up, tears him because they dislike his witty way of talking. King Henry IV best expresses the confused and dark view of past and future seen by most of Shakespeare's characters in the midst of history:

> O God, that one might read the book of fate,
> And see the revolution of the times
> Make mountains level, and the continent,
> Weary of solid firmness, melt itself
> Into the sea! And other times to see
> The beachy girdle of the ocean
> Too wide for Neptune's hips. How chances, mocks,

And changes fill the cup of alteration
With divers liquors! O, if this were seen,
The happiest youth, viewing his progress through,
What perils past, what crosses to ensue,
Would shut the book, and sit him down and die.

(*2 Henry IV*, 3.1.45-56)

Such a conception of man's inability to understand history while he is in the midst of it does not mean that the poet-historian who stands outside the events cannot have a meaningful overview, but it does suggest that he does not conceive of history in the clear precise patterns of universal historians like Gibbon, or Marx, or Toynbee, but rather senses it, more like Carlyle, as a swirling and confused movement in uncertain directions, which might best be described as a myth, or even a pageant, rather than as an abstract and analytical theory of history. That pageant appears in its most concentrated and complete form, not in the history plays proper, but in the tragedy *King Lear*, and I would now like to use that play, gathering around it events and characters from other plays, to trace the general outlines of Shakespeare's pageant of history.

The pageant regularly begins with the presentation of an old order, often centered on a legitimate king, for instance, Old Hamlet, Priam, Richard II, Lear, Duncan, but sometimes figured as a ruler whose legitimacy is more questionable, like Bolingbroke, Henry V, Edward IV, or even Julius Caesar, or sometimes represented by an established political body, like the Venetian Senate in *Othello* or the Triumvirate in *Antony and Cleopatra*. The essential qualities of this established order are manifest in King Lear, "every inch a king," a man who has in his countenance that authority which his followers "would fain call master." As Professor Danson puts it in his lecture, where he sees this quality at the center of *Lear*, the king is massive, a natural force who "seems less a victim than another aspect of the wind and rain and thunder and spouting hurricanoes in which he hugely exists." Lear is a kingly personage in his own right, a "natural ruler" we would say,

15

powerful, strong-willed, commanding, courageous, aristocratic in every way; and his natural right to rule, i.e. his
personal power, is reinforced by custom and legitimacy. He
is an old king, as old a man, "fourscore and upward," and
as old a king, being one of the legendary kings of ancient
Britain, as Shakespeare can make him. He is as "wrinkled
deep" in kingship as Cleopatra is in time. He gathers around
him all the ceremonies, the values, the trappings, and the
extended family of the old social order—the court fool
(Charles I was the last English monarch to have a court fool),
the private army of knights, the servants faithful unto death,
the attendant lords of the realm.

In Lear and his court, Shakespeare characteristically con-
flates elements of British mythology, medieval feudalism, and
Renaissance benevolent despotism to create a composite image of an older order, which exists in mystic communion with
God, with the order of the cosmos, and with a land whose
sacredness is best described, in another play, by John of Gaunt
at the moment when it is being violated by a new attitude of
exploitation for profit:

> This royal throne of kings, this scept'red isle,
> This earth of majesty, this seat of Mars,
> This other Eden, demi-paradise,
> This fortress built by Nature for herself
> Against infection and the hand of war,
> This happy breed of men, this little world,
> This precious stone set in the silver sea . . .
>
> . . . .
>
> Is now leased out—I die pronouncing it—
> Like to a tenement or pelting farm.
> (*Richard II*, 2.1.40-60)

This Edenic old kingdom always has in itself some fatal vulnerability and is always, even as it appears at the beginning
of the plays, passing, as in John of Gaunt's deathbed speech.
Either its old kings are too innocent to defend themselves
against reality, like Old Hamlet or Duncan, or their vanity
misleads them, like Julius Caesar, or they fail to understand

the practical realities on which their power rests, like Richard II, or they are too absorbed in their own private concerns, like Prospero when he was Duke of Milan in *The Tempest*. Shakespeare approaches the event from many different angles, but always the old order begins to crumble because of its own internal weakness. The essential nature of this original weakness is revealed in Lear, who destroys his world by giving away his land, banishing his friends and those who love him, and putting his power into the hands of the selfish and the wicked. His motives are too numerous for certainty (a desire to be loved and praised publicly, seeking his own ease in early retirement, susceptibility to flattery), but the basic trouble is clearly articulated by his daughter Regan: "he hath ever but slenderly known himself." The implications of this perception are explored with remarkable sensitivity and precision in Michael Goldman's lecture, which shows that the gap between Lear's feelings and his actions is the central problem for the actor in the part and an expression of the central theme of the play. The old order is always breached because the kings who are its chief symbols and defenders lack true knowledge of what they are, and misunderstand in some fatal way the realities on which they and their society ultimately depend.

Once the kings have unbarred the gates to their castles, there is a multitude waiting outside to pour in and destroy the old order: feudal barons like the Earl of Northumberland and his son Hotspur; Welsh, Scottish, Norwegian, and Turkish raiders; rising gentry like Macbeth; power-seeking churchmen like the Archbishop of York or Cardinal Wolsey; rebellious peasants like Jack Cade; disaffected soldiers like Iago; Byzantine palace conspirators like Claudius; or aristocratic idealistic revolutionaries like Brutus. Modern historians looking backward see the crucial political issue of Shakespeare's age as the new struggle between the aristocracy and the middle class that eventually produced the modern state, but in Shakespeare's view of history the antagonists of the old aristocratic order belong to no particular social class or religious or political persuasion. They form a gallery of all the many historical types, conservative and radical, old and new, rich and poor, insiders and outsiders, who threatened the Elizabethan compromise. They are united, however, by a characteristic way of thinking about and approaching life, an ethos that was at the root of most of the political and social changes that were to come in 1642, 1688, and 1832. That ethos and the old aristocratic way of life it opposes in Shakespeare differ in detail but not in essence from the ethical polarities of the age as described by a modern historian:

> The capitalist Protestant ethic is one of self-improvement, independence, thrift, hard work, chastity and sobriety, competition, equality of opportunity, and the association of poverty with moral weakness; the aristocratic ethic is one of voluntary service to the State, generous hospitality, clear class distinctions, social stability, tolerant indifference to the sins of the flesh, inequality of opportunity based on the accident of inheritance, arrogant self-confidence, a paternalist and patronizing attitude towards economic dependants and inferiors, and an acceptance of the grinding poverty of the lower classes as part of the natural order of things. If in this age of confusion and turmoil many men—even Cromwell himself—seem to straddle the two ideals, this does nothing to minimize the essential contradiction between them.[5]

Edmund, the illegitimate son of the Duke of Gloucester in *King Lear*, is Shakespeare's summary image of the new ethos, and his bastardy suggests the relationship of these new men to the traditional order: they are not usually barbarian invaders from the outside, but the manifestation of certain illegitimate tendencies and uncontrolled natural appetites within the old order itself. Edmund's famous soliloquy on nature summarizes the point of view of the Shakespearean new men, who see the proper life of a man, not as the observation of traditional rules of conduct and maintaining their station in a hierarchical society, but as a struggle in which the strongest, the most intelligent, the handsomest, the most courageous,

[5] Ibid., p. 6.

the most vital, and the most active and ruthless seize land and
power from the weaker and less intelligent.

> Thou, Nature, art my goddess; to thy law
> My services are bound. Wherefore should I
> Stand in the plague of custom, and permit
> The curiosity of nations to deprive me,
> For that I am some twelve or fourteen moonshines
> Lag of a brother? Why bastard? Wherefore base?
> When my dimensions are as well compact,
> My mind as generous, and my shape as true,
> As honest madam's issue? Why brand they us
> With base? With baseness? Bastardy? Base? Base?
> Who, in the lusty stealth of nature, take
> More composition and fierce quality
> Than doth, within a dull, stale, tired bed,
> Go to th' creating a whole tribe of fops
> Got 'tween asleep and wake? Well then,
> Legitimate Edgar, I must have your land.

$$(1.2.1-16)$$

The nature to which Edmund and others of his kind give
allegiance is not the old nature of love and obedience but the
new nature, "nature red in tooth and claw," of Hobbes and
Darwin. It has many different forms in Shakespearean drama:
as self-centered and individualistic as Richard III—"Richard
loves Richard: that is, I am I"; as rationalistic as Brutus working out why Caesar must bleed, or Claudius explaining to
Hamlet that the death of fathers is a commonplace of nature;
as antisuperstitious as Hotspur mocking old Glendower's
claims to be able to call spirits from the vasty deep, or Edmund
laughing at his father's belief in astrology; as humorously
practical as Falstaff's parodies of high political rhetoric and
the attitudes of chivalry, or as cynically practical as Iago's
advice to Roderigo on how to win Desdemona—"Go, put
money in thy purse." The essence of these attitudes is often
best expressed in brief but remarkably startling lines that go
to the very center of things, like Lady Macbeth's, "a little
water clears us of this deed"; or Regan's words to King Lear:

"I pray you, father, being weak seem so"; or Iago's comment on Desdemona: "Blessed fig's-end! The wine she drinks is made of grapes"; or Octavius Caesar's cool response to Antony's challenge to single combat: "let the old ruffian know I have many other ways to die."

Shakespearean drama is extremely ambivalent toward these rational, hardheaded, self-seeking new men and women. Even at their worst they always speak a kind of hard truth, and their energy, daring, and practical political skills always command dramatic if not moral admiration. At their best they can enlist our sympathies almost entirely, as does a Falstaff whose reduction of the world to pleasure and pain (the one to be sought, the other to be avoided) makes a kind of obvious good sense; or a Brutus seeking to act upon the most rational grounds for what he believes to be the good of the state; even, perhaps, a Macbeth whose rebellion and murders lead him to a deep knowledge of himself and of human nature that is not approached by anyone else in the play, except his wife, who draws back from it into madness. It is these men and women who make Shakespearean drama go, who are, like Milton's Satan, whom they resemble, the driving energies of the world in which they live. But in Shakespeare's historical world they always have a catastrophic effect on the old social order. Its crucial rituals, like trial by combat in *Richard II* and the duel in *Hamlet*, are destroyed; its law breaks down as in *The Merchant of Venice* and *Measure for Measure*; its knights like Coriolanus, or Hector, or the French chivalry at Agincourt die before superior powers; its central customs such as primogeniture are perverted in Elsinore. With its destruction of families (described by Professor McFarland) and kingdom, the betrayal of all human relationships, the old and the helpless turned out and delivered to the torturer, *King Lear* presents Shakespeare's ultimate image of the horror of the world of pure power that follows on the breakdown of the old kingdom:

Love cools, friendship falls off, brothers divide. In cities, mutinies; in countries, discord; in palaces, treason; and

the bond cracked 'twixt son and father. . . . We have seen
the best of our time. Machinations, hollowness, treach-
ery, and all ruinous disorders follow us disquietly to our
graves.

(1.2.109-117)

Shakespeare's central symbol in *King Lear* for this condition
at which the old kingdom arrives as a result of its own weakness and the rebellious forces it looses on itself is the heath
in the darkness of a great storm. Here in its most elemental
form is the mandatory scene toward which Shakespearean
history always moves, the point at which man faces the realities of the world stripped of all pretenses and all the protective
covering provided by a society, its rituals and its roles. This
crucial scene takes many forms in Shakespeare's historical
plays: Richard II in the dungeon of Pomfret Castle trying to
puzzle out his loss of identity; Brutus trying to persuade the
Roman mob that the death of Caesar was for the good of the
state; Hamlet in the graveyard holding the skull of Yorick in
his hand; Henry V talking with his soldiers in the light of the
flickering fires on the eve of the battle of Agincourt; Antony
realizing that the empire is lost and seeing in the moving,
changing clouds the image of the endless mutability of the
world, "That which is now a horse, even with a thought / The
rack dislimns, and makes it indistinct / As water is in water"
(4.14.9-11). Here in this type of scene we find what is most
distinctive and radical in Shakespeare's conception of history,
for it brings men into direct confrontation with the ultimate
reality on which individual life and political and social structures finally rest.

As I suggested earlier, that reality is never clear or revelatory
of some transcendent order, but always problematic and
doubtful. This is nowhere more clearly seen than in *Lear*,
where life is reduced on the heath to a maddened old man,
stripped naked, accompanied by a fool, a few faithful followers, and a ragged, crazed beggar, wandering aimlessly across
a bleak wasteland in the midst of a dreadful storm that pities
neither man nor beast. If the old gods are present here, they

do not reveal themselves. Seen without covering, the world seems to offer justification for nothing, to be only a terrible place of struggle, and suffering, and emptiness. But the men who experience this fearsome view of nature come to feel, not to understand rationally, some sense of community and bond among themselves. Shakespearean history offers no absolute basis on which to authenticate any view of kingship, government, or society, but it does force men to see that, if any human society or set of values is to exist in the face of that inhuman world, then it must be put together by men. Out of their pity and feeling for the sufferings of one another they must show the heavens more just, without any metaphysical support. Just government is in Shakespeare a human ideal, and community a human value, not inevitable fact, and they depend finally on human feelings, not on rational thought.

In Shakespeare's treatment of history, the discovery that the human community and the state lack any absolute metaphysical underpinnings is experienced in many different ways and with many different results. Faced with the irrationality of the Roman mob, Brutus takes refuge in Stoicism, flies to Greece, and leaves the state to the tyranny of the Triumvirate; Richard II, after seeing the absurdity of his belief that he stands to the state as God does to the world and the sun to the universe, dies, after a desperate attempt to hammer out a new world, in a sudden surge of violence; Henry V locks himself in the isolation of a round of endless ceremonies of state in which the man is transformed into a political function. But in general the experience of the void underlying history, though catastrophic for the individuals who see it, sets the world on the road toward a partial rebuilding of society. In *King Lear*, those who escape the heath gradually find in their own need and in their reawakened capability for sympathy with their fellows the grounds for a reconstitution of the social world, which manifests itself first in the reunion of families, Lear with his daughter Cordelia, and Gloucester with his legitimate son Edgar, and then in a recomposition of society as the forces of evil are destroyed, or destroy themselves.

But it is not the old order that is restored at the end of the

Shakespearean historical pageant, but some greatly diminished and more limited thing. At the end of *Lear*, the old king, the very essence of traditional kingship, lies dead, and all his daughters dead before him. And although the kingdom has been restored to virtuous men, Edgar and the Duke of Albany, who have been thoroughly tested and toughened by their experience of the far ends of the world and the far reaches of human nature, there is a notable reluctance on the part of both to accept the crown and restore the kingdom. The ending of the play implies that the kingdom will go on, as it always does in Shakespeare, and that it is crucial that it should; but in the saddened knowledge of full reality it somehow does not matter as much as it once did. As each of the prospective rulers voices his reluctance to assume the throne, it becomes clear that government has become a heavy necessity and can no longer be thought of, as Richard II or King Lear once conceived of it, as a manifestation of the order of the universe and the natural instincts of men.

The conclusion of *Lear* precisely focuses Shakespeare's sense of historical endings. Somehow the world always rights itself and government is restored to the hands of men of justice, honor, and a feeling of community, not left—except perhaps in the case of Octavius Caesar in both *Julius Caesar* and *Antony and Cleopatra*—in the hands of men who understand only power and self-advancement. Richard II dies, but the strong and effective ruler Henry V eventually comes to the throne; Hamlet kills Claudius and young Fortinbras wears the crown; Scotland casts out Macbeth and takes young Malcolm for its king; and Prospero returns eventually to Milan and his dukedom. But, as these examples suggest, it is never the same again. The joy, the grandeur, the enormous certainty of the earlier world is gone, and the rulers who stand at the end of the historical process are usually diminished, always more uneasy and uncertain, than those they succeed. Shakespearean history is not cyclical but linear, not a glorious return after a period of trouble to the Edenic garden, but, as in *Lear*, an enormous historical pageant in which the Middle Ages move on into the modern world as kings of almost supernatural power move in regal procession across the stage, surrounded by their courts and families, accompanied by their brave knights and proud captains, decked in all the ancient symbols of their authority:

> the balm, the scepter, and the ball,
> The sword, the mace, the crown imperial,
> The intertissued robe of gold and pearl,
> The farcèd title running 'fore the king,
> The throne he sits on . . . the tide of pomp
> That beats upon the high shore of this world—
> *(Henry V,* 4.1.260-265)

But as the pageant of kingship passes on, family and court fall away, its ceremonies become ineffective "maimed rites," its gods do not answer its invocations, and the king, stripped of all the protective coverings of society, is left alone to look directly at the bare fact of man:

> Is man no more than this? Consider him well. Thou ow'st the worm no silk, the beast no hide, the sheep no wool, the cat no perfume. . . . Thou art the thing itself; unaccommodated man is no more but such a poor, bare, forked animal as thou art.
>
> *(King Lear,* 3.4.102-107)

It is the measure of Shakespeare's optimism that his pageant of history does not end in this bleak and totally reductive vision of a world that pities neither man nor beast, but moves relentlessly on into the future where "the art of our necessities" fashions new coverings and new political and social accommodations. But to any exclamations of joy, such as Miranda's "O brave new world / That has such people in't!" the plays seem always to answer with Prospero for an old kingdom lost forever in the past, " 'Tis new to thee."

Two

King Lear:
Acting and Feeling

Michael Goldman

I am going to talk today about what might be called the histrionic imagery of *King Lear*. What I have in mind when I use that phrase are various motifs Shakespeare has built into the leading role. These are motifs of enactment: mental, physical, and emotional movements the actor is called upon to make that are particularly related to his basic work of sustaining the part in performance. I am interested both in the typical acting problems Shakespeare sets the actor and the typical means he provides for solving them.

Let me try to give an example of what I mean. The first problem that confronts an actor who wants to play Lear is gross and obvious. The part makes staggering emotional demands on the performer. The actor is required to portray a quick-tempered, eighty-year-old, absolute tyrant, who five minutes into his first scene bursts into the greatest rage of his life at Cordelia. Two brief scenes later he bursts into a greater rage at Goneril and carries on with increasing intensity for nearly a hundred lines. Next he gets *really* angry at Regan; while he is raging at her, Goneril appears and he gets angrier. His fury and outrage mount wildly until the end of the scene, at which point he goes mad. This of course is only the beginning. Three long scenes of madness still lie ahead during which, among other things, the actor has to outshout a storm. After these scenes on the heath come alternations of hallucination and murderous rage in the scene with Gloucester, the ecstatic joy of reunion with Cordelia, yet another reversal of fortune when the old king and his daughter are captured by their enemies, and finally the anguish of Cordelia's death, a scene in which the actor is required to enter literally howling and to go on from there. "The wonder is," as Kent says, "he hath endured so long," and most actors don't.

The actor who plays Lear must appear to reach an emotional extreme at the start, and then go on to greater and greater extremes. The danger is that he will soon have nothing left, not so much that he won't have voice or physical energy, but that he will have no capacity for discriminating his emotional response, that he will be unable to render the emotions truthfully, with freshness and particularity, and will fall into shouting or scenery chewing or playing what actors call generalized emotion, that is, some sort of all-purpose posturing. If this happens, the actor will not only be doing a great injustice to the text, he will also in a matter of moments bore his audience irremediably. Does Shakespeare do anything to help the actor with this problem?

Trained actors usually learn a variety of techniques for sustaining exact and vivid emotion in scenes of demanding intensity. One technique is to focus on a particular object. If the actor feels in danger of losing an emotion or falsifying it, he may single out a button, say, or a chair, or an eyebrow and make it the recipient or evoker of his feeling. He may direct his emotion toward the object, or find his emotion by reacting to it. In *King Lear* Shakespeare has written this technique into the title role. Repeatedly, at moments of emotional intensity, Lear will focus closely on a specific point—on an area of the body and its sensation or on a small object that produces a bodily sensation. He takes a pin and pricks himself with it; he feels the pressure of a button at his throat; he pinches himself; he holds a feather to Cordelia's mouth; he peers at Gloucester's blinded eyes; he touches Cordelia's cheek to feel the wetness of her tears; he glares at Regan's and Goneril's clasped hands; he smells and wipes his own hand; he imagines two little flies copulating; he stares at Cordelia's lips. These are all highly specific points of focus, and by playing to them and *off* them the actor is able to keep his feeling fresh. They help him to keep the performance alive, to keep the pain Lear feels coming and growing, and to keep the audience's perception of that pain vivid and exact.

These recurring gestures or movements of focus are an example of what I call histrionic images. If we were simply to consider the objects Lear focuses on by themselves, we might treat them as what are usually called poetic or dramatic images. But I am concerned with a unit of *enactment*, something Shakespeare has prescribed for the character to do, by means of which the actor projects the part. Hence, it is this repeated focusing on an area of bodily sensation that constitutes one pattern of histrionic imagery in *Lear*.

Having explained my subject, perhaps I should say something about why histrionic images are worth studying. With few exceptions, our experience of any play—our entire sense of its action or meaning—comes from what we see its actors doing, that is, from acting, because acting is almost all we see and hear in the theater. This means that there will always be a significant connection between these local motifs of acting—the building blocks of performance, the small individual bits of process by which the actor keeps his projection of the character alive and interesting—and the larger action of the play, just as there is a connection between the brush stroke of Rembrandt and the felt significance of his design, or between the imagery of a poem and whatever meaning or value we find in it.

Any analysis of a great play must take into account the defining problems of its major parts, the sense of difficulty overcome that their performance conveys, because this inevitably influences our experience of the play. For instance, the problem of human suffering is clearly one of the issues *King Lear* raises. Why do we suffer? Is there anything to be gained from it? What values can be conserved in the face of monstrous pain? These are questions the characters keep posing or addressing. And the action is designed so that we frequently find ourselves, like Edgar, believing that things cannot get any worse, only to have something happen that is more awful than anything else that has happened so far. The play's interest in suffering and endurance is plainly echoed in the problem of playing Lear and in our reaction to the performance of the role. How much more can the actor take? we ask—and the question implies, How much more can we take? A good production of *Lear* is not easy on its audience.

Now, the sequence of repeated focusings I have just described may be seen as part of the play's subtle and growing insistence on *feeling* as a source of enduring value in the chaos of cruelty and pain that threatens to overwhelm the characters, the actors, and the audience. The function of these histrionic images is, not to insist on a theme, but to engage the audience in an experience. That is, through the action of the principal actor we share the experience of discovering new precisions of feeling—moments of sympathy, tenderness, insight, or horror, for example—in spite of and indeed because of being forced to undergo scenes that strike us as unendurable and that threaten to wipe us out. They give us the sensation of advancing deeper into pain than we thought we could take, and of advancing, not into generalized empty agitation or monotony, but into profounder awareness, finer sensitivity, which could only be achieved by going this far, by having these many stages of exact response to increasing pain. And this I think is a not insignificant part of the art and vision of *King Lear*.

I would like now to look at some other patterns of histrionic imagery, in which the actor is called upon to address himself to other characters, to the words he speaks, and above all to his own emotions. I want especially to draw your attention to the emotional and intellectual activity that all these motifs require of the actor and communicate to the audience. For, by means of these devices, Shakespeare provides the gifted actor with a set of habits and methods that allow him to relate to his own emotions, to build them, vary them, wield them, and, as we have seen, to keep them from turning imprecise or numb. This is particularly important in *Lear* because Lear's own relation to his emotional life is one of the great problems of the play.

We tend to think of *Lear* as a play about human suffering, and we are right to do so. The play deliberately overwhelms us with examples of suffering that arouse our own most vivid fears of vulnerability to pain. How easy it is for our eyes to be put out, how easy it would be for the ones we trust most to betray us, how easily nature or the appetites of others can destroy us, how true it is that things can always get worse. But from the point of view of the enacted character of Lear, the play is concerned less with his suffering attack from the outside than with his vulnerability to the play of his own emotions.

In the early scenes, for example, Lear seems peculiarly agitated by the connections between the self and its acts. Indeed, like many of Shakespeare's tragic heroes, Lear seems inclined to work out a personal, abnormal variation on the process that links thinking and feeling with saying and doing. For Hamlet and Brutus, this variation takes the form of a desire to separate the two components, to divide one's inner life from its external manifestations—to insist with Brutus on separating what he calls the "genius" from the "mortal instruments," or with Hamlet that whatever one's acts may be, one has something within which passeth show. Lear on the other hand insists on intention and action as monolithically connected and on defining his own nature as powerfully and dangerously joining the two. He denounces Kent for attempting to break the connection when Kent tries to persuade him to revoke his decision to disinherit Cordelia, and he uses language that insists on the leap from self to action as something violent, powerful, instantaneous and irresistible:

> Come not between the dragon and his wrath. . . .
> The bow is bent and drawn; make from the shaft.

Like Macbeth, Lear seems unwilling or afraid to slow down the rhythm by which he moves from intention to act. Macbeth frequently wishes to act quickly in order to escape from his moral imagination. He would like to act the things in his head before he can scan them; he wants the firstlings of his heart to be the firstlings of his hand. Action for him is a way to blot out reflection and feeling. And the question of feeling, in particular, is important for both *Macbeth* and *King Lear*. Macbeth's desire to leap forward unreflectingly into action is highlighted by contrast with Macduff. After Macduff has heard that his wife and children have been murdered, he pauses before calling for revenge. He does so because, as he explains, in order to dispute it like a man, he first must feel it as a man. Macduff insists on the importance of feeling in a man's life, while Macbeth, concerned with doing all that may become a man, acts to keep from feeling. Similarly Lear, up to the storm scene, clings like Macbeth to an idea of a manly way of acting that seals one off from feeling. Confronting Regan and Goneril before Gloucester's palace, Lear, fighting against tears, calls on the gods to visit him instead with what he calls noble anger, a feeling he thinks of as more masculine:

> touch me with noble anger,
> And let not women's weapons, waterdrops,
> Stain my man's cheeks.
>
> (2.4.273-275)

I imagine that the kind of anger he wants here is the type he displayed in the first scene. He is struggling to summon once more his old power to discharge violent emotional energy without suffering the full range of feeling from which his emotion springs.

Indeed, almost from the beginning of the play, Lear is fighting his feelings. Shakespeare's method of allowing the actor to play against his feelings, by repeatedly insisting, for example, that he will not weep, allows us to experience the movement of feeling toward expression as a terrifying, destructive surge. We feel it as Lear's speeches swiftly shift focus in his fight against rising sorrow:

> O, how this mother swells up toward my heart!
> Hysterica passio, down, thou climbing sorrow,
> Thy element's below. Where is this daughter?
>
> (2.4.55-57)

With this last line, he switches attention to Regan, trying to direct action and anger outward, as he has done in the first scene.

Significantly, Lear is aware in this struggle of something unnatural, but he projects it onto his daughters as he flounders in a feeling so violent and unregulated that he cannot think clearly enough even to curse or invent a revenge:

> No, you unnatual hags!
> I will have such revenges on you both
> That all the world shall—I will do such things—
> What they are, yet I know not; but they shall be
> The terrors of the earth.
>
> (2.4.275-279)

The power of this speech goes quite beyond its pathos, its picture of a poor old man dissolving in misery yet, like a small boy, refusing to show tears. For, in a kind of prelude to the battle with the storm that comes in the next act, Lear in battling against the mounting tears reaches into himself for a terrifying violence with which to combat them. The long-delayed onslaught of tears, the surrender to his feelings, comes on with the first noise of the storm, and it is so strong that it feels as if he were breaking into a hundred thousand pieces:

> You think I'll weep.
> No, I'll not weep.
>
> *Storm and tempest.*
>
> I have full cause of weeping, but this heart
> Shall break into a hundred thousand flaws
> Or ere I'll weep.
>
> (2.4.279-283)

The actor's emotional springboard for this outburst must be found in his fight against tears, while the image of the heart breaking into a hundred thousand flaws gives him his cue for how immense the pressure of the choked back tears must be. And now comes a dramatic stroke, very helpful to the actor, that is also an important development in the part. Unable to beat back the surge of his emotions, Lear suddenly turns his attention outside again, not to curse and rage, but to confess: "O Fool, I shall go mad!" (2.4.283). At the moment of his strongest feeling and his deepest fear, he addresses the Fool. The Fool has already become associated with the kind of feeling Lear has been resisting, that is, with acknowledged suffering. His main role has been to urge the unpalatable, shaming truth that Lear has made a terrible mistake about his daughters. And to Lear, someone who weeps is a fool: "Fool me not so much," he has said in this scene, "to bear it tamely," that is, to weep. At this moment, the sudden focus on the Fool allows the actor to let Lear's suppressed feelings flash out for an instant, and the pattern of emotional release through a sudden external focus of attention will grow in importance as the play goes on. A few minutes later, out in the storm, it will be to the Fool that Lear will turn when, for the first time in the play, he acknowledges that someone else can suffer. It is thus through Lear's relation to the Fool that we first begin to feel how the experience of his own pain is converting into keener awareness of the life around him.

For the actor who plays Lear, the problem of handling Lear's emotions is inseparable from the problem of speaking the play's verse. A great deal of study has been devoted to the verse of Shakespeare's plays, but very little to verse movement and texture as part of the performance design. I mean that any striking instance of technical virtuosity in a play's verse will, if the actor can master it, inevitably present itself as technical virtuosity in performance. At this point I want to call attention to some features of the verse that Lear speaks in order to examine what actions they require of the actor. Since they are actions of speech, they will of course involve not simply vocal but also mental and emotional movement.

Lear himself has many styles of speech, many voices, more than I can investigate here. There is, for example, the riddling, shadowy voice we hear very briefly at the beginning of the play,

Meantime we will express our darker purpose.

> . . . while we
> Unburthened crawl toward death.
> (1.1.36, 40-41)

or the torrent of monosyllables in

> I will have such revenges on you both
> That all the world shall—I will do such things—
> What they are, yet I know not; but they shall be
> The terrors of the earth.
> (2.4.276-279)

or the eerie flickering lightness of the aria that begins "We two alone will sing like birds i' th' cage" (5.3.9ff.), not to mention the various voices that mingle in the prose of his madness.

Still, all these voices have one element in common: their suggestion of the operation of some dangerously unregulable power, something not quite contained by the procedures that seek to organize it. And this is equally true of a far more prominent stylistic effect that I wish to look at in some detail. This is the presence, both in Lear's part and in others, of words and phrases that appear to be massively resistant to verse articulation, words like "tender-hefted" or "sea-monster" or "sulph'rous," which seem hard to move around in musical lines or paragraphs. What we appreciate in the music of the lines in which they appear is that the lines somehow find an energy capable of floating or swinging these densely recalcitrant chunks of meaning and sound. Of course it is really the relation of such words to the words around them that creates the impression of difficulty, just as it creates the impression of difficulty overcome. Thus, when we hear:

> Thou art a boil,
> A plague-sore, or embossèd carbuncle
> In my corrupted blood.
> (2.4.220-222)

or "Strike flat the thick rotundity o' th' world" (3.2.7), we feel that somehow words hard to move are being moved.

33

These words often carry a suggestion of—let me call it—monstrosity, that is, they contribute, through sound and sense, to an impression of sizable, distorted, appetitive, struggling bodies; they burgeon against the forward career of the line:

> If thou shouldst not be glad,
> I would divorce me from thy mother's tomb,
> Sepulchring an adultress.
> (2.4.127-129)

They seem to overflow, like an unexpected wet animal coming out of a river to snap or lap or slaver at you, or to block your path as the line goes by. Sometimes this impression is specifically carried by the sense of the word itself, sometimes by the context, frequently by a thick play of consonants:

> The barbarous Scythian,
> Or he that makes his generation messes
> To gorge his appetite, shall to my bosom
> Be as well neighbored, pitied, and relieved,
> As thou my sometime daughter.[1]
> (1.1.116-120)

The movement of this passage is relatively easy, but, even so, the texture is quite unlike, say, that of Othello's equally savage but fast-moving curses or denunciations:

> Blow me about in winds! roast me in sulfur!
> Wash me in steep-down gulfs of liquid fire!
> (5.2.279-280)

In *Lear*, this characteristic texture is frequently achieved by using series of words linked by clashing consonants:

> If she must teem,
> Create her child of spleen, that it may live
> And be a thwart disnatured torment to her.
> Let it stamp wrinkles in her brow of youth,

[1] Note how, in this passage, "relieve," "pity," and "neighbor," words that carry an opposite sense to monstrosity or violence, take on, by management as well as by context, a resistant, snarling texture.

With cadent tears fret channels in her cheeks.
(1.4.283-287)

Lear usually sounds remarkably different from other Shakespearean tragic heroes, even in such a simple matter as a brief
explosion of rage. Take a line like "Vengeance! Plague! Death!
Confusion!" (2.4.92). Othello typically bursts out on a single
note of fury or revulsion: "Goats and monkeys!" or "O Devil,
devil!" or "Damn her, lewd minx, damn her!" Hamlet, even
in his rage, uses language that multiplies distinctions in series
of swiftly linked analytical variations:

Bloody, bawdy villain!
Remorseless, treacherous, lecherous, kindless villain!
(2.2.586-587)

Lear instead breaks out in four successive, sharply separated
calls for sweeping violence. Each is different, each involves,
as it were, a going back to the beginning and imagining a
new, more violent outbreak of destruction: "Vengeance!
Plague! Death! Confusion!"

We can now see some of the characteristic action of performance that this verse texture requires of the actor. Put
simply, the testing necessity is for the actor to maintain a
precision of feeling and an architecture of response that allows
him to swing through the line without falling into rant. To
some extent this is a quality any actor must achieve in any
passage of intense emotion, but here it is the dominant quality,
the one on which the greatest demand is made. Different roles
stress different demands. Again the comparison with Hamlet
is helpful. The problem with the lines from *Hamlet* I quoted
a few moments ago is that, by contrast with *Lear*, it is all too
easy to make them superficially musical and thus to lose the
play of distinctions and contrasts the words imply in the rapid,
nicely modulated interplay of their sounds. Everywhere in the
role of Hamlet, the actor's testing difficulty is to impose a
meaningful coherence on materials that are various, changing,
subtly differentiated, and quick moving. The part, like the
play, stresses the problems of *interpretation*, of making sense

out of a prolific tangle of human actions and motives. Indeed, this is what Hamlet is most concerned with when he instructs the players on how to perform in scenes of strong emotion. What he urges on them is interpretive control—temperance, smoothness, holding the mirror up to nature, showing virtue her feature and scorn her image. And even here, Hamlet's language echoes his analytical bent and sets for the actor the basic problem of bringing interpretive order out of variety. For when he describes emotional agitation as the "very torrent, tempest, and (as I may say) whirlwind of your passion," the actor must be at pains to do justice to this volley of interesting distinctions, with their mixture of playfulness, urgency, and critical reflection, while still holding the speech and the scene together and speaking it all trippingly upon the tongue. As in *Lear*, the acting of these passages is part of the fundamental action of the play.

The verse texture I have been talking about in *Lear* makes its greatest demands upon the actor when Lear confronts the storm in act 3:

> Blow, winds, and crack your cheeks. Rage, blow!
> (3.2.1)

These words are resistant. Each threatens to stop the line dead, to exhaust or baffle the actor's power to articulate. There is no easy musical way to link them. The consonants clash, the vowels expand. It is hard to move from "blow" to "winds" and to get up further energy for "crack your cheeks"; then there are two more imperatives to go, and that's just the first line. For of course the speech continues:

> Blow, winds, and crack your cheeks. Rage, blow!
> You cataracts and hurricanoes, spout
> Till you have drenched our steeples, drowned the cocks.
> You sulph'rous and thought-executing fires,
> Vaunt-couriers of oak-cleaving thunderbolts,
> Singe my white head. And thou, all-shaking thunder,
> Strike flat the thick rotundity o' th' world.
> (3.2.1-7)

The actor's problem here is to maintain some movement of thought and articulation that will carry him through the dead stopping explosions of "rage" and "blow" and on to the other unwieldy, massively active words.

It should be noted, too, that the effort of speech required here echoes Lear's complex relation to the storm. Lear fights the storm, but he also uses it as a means of releasing his own feelings. He claims later that the tempest in his mind keeps him from noticing the tempest around him, but this is plainly inaccurate. For it is through Lear's dialogue with the storm that the audience becomes aware of the tempest in his mind, and it is by playing to the storm that Lear confronts his emotions.

In the speech I have just quoted, Lear is once more attempting to establish the connection between himself and the outside world he has desperately tried to maintain throughout the play. That is, under the stress of his own torment and shame, he again tries to thrust any source of emotional disturbance away from him by uttering angry commands. But now the emotion that is wracking him is so great that it can only be uttered, that is, projected outward, as a total destruction of nature, a cracking of nature's molds, and the effort required to project it outward is captured by the actor's effort to address the storm. The vocal effort needed to get from "blow" to "winds" and so on embodies this, for it is like trying to reach up and touch the storm, to become the thunder and the wind. The storm is significantly called "thought-executing," for in it we feel the explosive release of the thoughts Lear can no longer keep down.

Lear's relation to the storm swings rapidly from commanding it to insulting it to holding his tongue again, and then he returns to identifying with the storm—but now no physical effort of emulation is involved. He is no longer acting out the storm but, as it were, imagining it. And he imagines it in terms of its effects on a population of hidden sinners:

> Tremble, thou wretch,
> That hast within thee undivulgèd crimes

Unwhipped of justice. Hide thee, thou bloody hand,
Thou perjured, and thou simular of virtue
That art incestuous. Caitiff, to pieces shake,
That under covert and convenient seeming
Has practiced on man's life.

(3.2.51-57)

Two points are interesting here. First, this is the first time in the play that Lear focuses on other individuals as centers of suffering. Second, Lear connects the active power of the storm with the eruption of hidden evil. The moral point here is less important than the psychological one. Lear suddenly is no longer talking about violence that comes from outside but about violence that bursts from within:

> Close pent-up guilts,
> Rive your concealing continents and cry
> These dreadful summoners grace.

(3.2.57-59)

This shift to erupting guilt makes the lines that follow—"I am a man / More sinned against than sinning" (3.2.59-60)—complex indeed. For Lear is moved to protest his relative innocence, not by thoughts of what he is being subjected to, but by thoughts of guilt bursting out. What he suffers seems bound up in his mind with guilt, guilt associated with sexual crimes and murder. Perhaps he experiences the force of his emotions as murderous and sexually irregular. The actor can find the emotional life that keeps this scene from degenerating into rant only by carefully charting how Lear's rapidly varying attack on the storm follows the surges of that inner suffering he now begins to acknowledge. He rives his own concealing continents to do so.

It is at this point that Lear says his wits are turning, and suddenly directs his attention to yet another center of suffering. This time it is a real person, not an imagined throng of sinners. He becomes aware that the Fool is cold, comforts him, and admits that he is cold himself. Out of this immense, chaotic explosion of long-denied emotion comes a moment of minute, concrete, ordinary feeling, a tenderness we have not seen before, based on an acknowledgment of shared pain.

> My wits begin to turn.
> Come on, my boy. How dost, my boy? Art cold?
> I am cold myself.

(3.2.67-69)

These moments of awareness and tenderness become an important motif in the play as Lear directs his new capacity for close attention to the naked wretches in the storm, to Edgar and, later, to Gloucester and Cordelia.

All the various motifs of performance I have been discussing have in common a demand placed on the actor—and a concomitant opportunity given him—to apprehend concrete, sharply defined foci of pain. They require that the actor keep *renewing* his sensations, opening himself to a particularity of suffering. The scene in act 4 during which Lear meets Gloucester and Edgar on the way to Dover is full of such histrionic patterns. There are several things on Lear's mind here: sexual loathing, revenge, a hallucinatory, at times satirical, vision of court life and of himself as king, a foollike insistence on unpleasant truths in his conversations with Gloucester, and at the same time a tenderness toward Gloucester's suffering. But in every case there is a marked movement of scrutiny—of Lear thrusting himself forward to examine some detail in its full vividness of sensation. Lear focuses at different moments on, among other things, Gloucester's blinded eyes, a mouse, a wren, a small fly, a man accused of adultery, Gloucester's tears, and finally on the hoofs of a troop of horses, shod with felt, pattering across the great stage of the Globe theater.

A few examples from this scene will show the histrionic imagery at work. At its beginning, Lear imagines himself as king. His hallucination projects a world whose dimensions are freely changing. The result is that Lear constantly seems to be on the scale of what he encounters, be it a mouse or a flying arrow or a troop of soldiers:

> That fellow handles his bow like a crow-keeper; draw
> me a clothier's yard. Look, look, a mouse! Peace, peace;
> this piece of toasted cheese will do't. There's my gauntlet;
> I'll prove it on a giant. Bring up the brown bills. O, well
> flown, bird! i' th' clout, i' th' clout: hewgh!
>
> (4.6.87-92)

The mental movement here is in striking contrast to Lear's
stance at the beginning of the play, where he insisted on control, on maintaining a scale through which he dominated. His
reference to the bow may recall his great image of irresistible
authority in the first scene ("The bow is bent and drawn;
make from the shaft"), but now he follows the shaft into the
target and mimes its whizzing sound. From the grand command to the thing commanded in an instant, from the straining
bow to the little mouse, this new lability is a measure of how
Lear has changed.

As the scene progresses, the sense of smell is emphasized,
competing with touch and sight for prominence. Sharply concrete references to smell and sexuality are mingled. The hand
that smells of mortality, the little gilded copulating fly, the
soiled horse, and above all the genitalia of women are on
Lear's mind, and he responds to them as if they sweated and
stank with a combination of sexual abandon and decay. Even
a description of virtue is charged with a grotesque prurience:

> Behold yond simp'ring dame,
> Whose face between her forks presages snow.
>
> (4.6.118-119)

The effect of the syntax is to displace a visual image of chastity
downward so sharply that it emerges as a grossly suggestive
image of sexual license, and leads Lear quickly to sensations
of burning and stench:

> But to the girdle do the gods inherit,
> Beneath is all the fiend's.
> There's hell, there's darkness, there is the sulphurous pit,
> burning, scalding, stench, consumption; fie, fie, fie! pah,
> pah!
>
> (4.6.126-130)

Lear's agony is immense. He has not yet emerged from the tempest in his mind, but now he is harrowed by vivid physical sensations, which he links to emotional disturbance, again, as in the third act, connecting them with sexual transgression. The denial of emotion, the association of unmanageable feeling with humiliating taint is still strong. Now, as Gloucester offers to kiss his hand, Lear imagines that Gloucester is squinting, peering at him perhaps lecherously. At any rate he associates Gloucester with the emblem of blind Cupid, which was sometimes hung as a sign above a brothel:

> Dost thou squiny at me? No, do thy worst, blind Cupid;
> I'll not love.
>
> (4.6.136-138)

He rejects love. More important, Lear connects love with the idea of painful scrutiny and does this by means of images that carry the force of the sexual revulsion he feels welling up inside him.

At the end of the scene between them, Lear continues to swing from one tack to another, from imagining a spectacle of injustice, full of specific physical images, to a tender awareness of Gloucester weeping, to the vividly imagined tightness of his probably nonexistent boots, and back to Gloucester:

> If thou wilt weep my fortunes, take my eyes.
> I know thee well enough; thy name is Gloucester:
> Thou must be patient; we came crying hither
> (4.6.176-178)

and thus to a sense of the entire career of human life as smelling, weeping, and playing the fool:

> Thou know'st, the first time that we smell the air
> We wawl and cry. . . .
> . . . .
>   We cry that we are come
> To this great stage of fools.
>
> (4.6.179-183)

Then suddenly he turns to revenge, but it too is conceived in terms of immediate sensation:

> It were a delicate stratagem, to shoe
> A troop of horse with felt. . . .
> And when I have stol'n upon these son-in-laws,
> Then, kill, kill, kill, kill, kill, kill!
>
> > (4.6.184-187)

This last line provides an example of another memorable feature of the play's verse—the accumulative pattern, the use of intensifying repetition, and it offers a final instance of how the action of the actor shapes the meaning of the play. For what is the histrionic problem set by lines like "kill, kill, kill, kill, kill, kill" and "Now, now, now, now" and "Never, never, never, never, never" and "Howl, howl, howl, howl"? In performance they act out a tension between the desire for absoluteness of response and the need for renewal, between the thrill of letting go, of crying out, and the labor of concentration, of finding a precise image for each exclamation in the series. Such lines long to be only a cry, but they must have a content or they go dead: they escape, as every audience and every critic longs to escape, from the dreadful particularity of the play. They too demand, and make possible, that regular renewal of sensation crucial to the role.

I want to shift perspective now and consider briefly a few of the ways in which Shakespeare locates the small acting patterns I have been talking about in what we experience as the larger world of the play. I will take as examples some features of Shakespeare's treatment of action and space.

In Shakespeare's tragedies we normally feel that the action proceeds from the interplay of some more or less controlled and steadily maintained personal or political schemes, for example, Hamlet versus Claudius, or Macbeth versus those he first displaces and later is overthrown by. Now, though it is equally easy to discern in *King Lear* the movements of warring parties whose fortunes swing up and down and though there is, when one reflects on it, a surprising amount of intrigue, public and private, in the play (the secret conference, scheming, suspicion, and letter writing that have always formed the staple of the drama of intrigue), our *impression* of the action of *King Lear* is likely to be more chaotic. All the scheming is felt to take place on the edge of a much larger disturbance (Kent and a gentleman exchanging secrets in the storm, Regan and Goneril hurriedly conferring after the first scene as the court breaks up in confusion, Oswald carrying letters back and forth while the world goes mad).

At the same time, a major activity in the play is expulsion: Lear expelling Cordelia and Kent; Goneril and Regan forcing Lear out into the storm; Edmund forcing Edgar to run away; Cornwall throwing out the blinded Gloucester. Even assistance is most often seen, not as taking someone in, but as helping someone get away to an unspecified or temporary location. Thus, the intrigue in the play communicates itself to us as a set of fragile strands of intention winding across a large and threatening outdoor space.

For the sense of space in *King Lear* is unique in the Shakespearean canon. Instead of being presented with the usual two or at most three major locales, we are in great part urged to think of the stage as representing a place en route. And these scenes are unlike the en route scenes of the histories or other plays that, like *Lear*, have battles in them, because in *Lear* they are felt to be not stages of access to a major location (Shrewsbury, Dunsinane), but rather pieces of a vast, unlocalized, transitional space, the large, exposed, generally inhospitable expanse of England. The largeness of Lear's England has been stressed in the early moments of the first scene, when Lear responds to Goneril and Regan's declarations of total love:

> Of all these bounds, even from this line to this,
> With shadowy forests, and with champains riched,
> With plenteous rivers, and wide-skirted meads,
> We make thee lady.
>
> (1.1.63-66)

But the greenness and richness of this world seem to vanish

with Cordelia's refusal and Lear's curse; only the largeness remains. After the initial explosion in the great, ordered presence chamber, the indoors of the play becomes little more than a series of ad hoc auxiliary confines—a hovel, a lodging, an outbuilding, some convenient, borrowed room for torture. The rest is outdoors, on the way, dust blown, wind-swept and bare, a space crisscrossed by the play's many frail and circuitous threads of intention: groups hurriedly quitting home, search parties, messengers, outlaws. We see letters moving about through curious and uncertain routes. Not only the messengers but the senders and recipients are on the move, and the letters are read not at leisure but under stress—in a storm, in the stocks, after a fight to the death. This sense of large, unorganized space and of errant, improvised movement through it is fundamental to the play, and helps locate Lear's recurrent focus upon minute particulars of sensation.

Lear's small gestures of scrutiny and physical contact stand out against the large, chaotic space of the play. And it is against the same background that we see one of the play's familiar sights—people supporting each other, one leading another by a hand or arm, two supporting one, one touching another. Edgar, Lear, and Gloucester seem to spend much of the play reeducating themselves in feeling through the exercise of touch, and this, too, adds to the impression of a fragile thread of feeling poised against the storm.

When Cordelia wakes Lear, he does not know whether or not he is alive. To see if he is, he pricks his skin with a pin. It is a basic test, whose meaning is central to the play. To be conscious is to be able to feel pain. Where there's life, there's hurt. Next Lear wants to know if Cordelia is real and human instead of a vision or an angel. He decides she is real when he notices her tears are wet. This tender concentration on the facts of pain takes on a special strength when we reach the play's final scene.

Lear's whole last sequence with Cordelia's body is a series of sharp focusings that insist on the unbearable distinction between life and death. Lear attends carefully to the looking glass, the feather, Cordelia's voice, her breath, her mouth. His eyes are not o' the best, but he makes an effort to scrutinize Kent's face. Then he asks someone to undo a button—at his own throat, I think—and turns back to stare at Cordelia's lips. His last words combine his three great modes of enactment—the giving of commands, intensification through repetition, scrutiny of particulars:

> Look on her. Look, her lips,
> Look there, look there.
>
> (5.3.312-313)

There is also in this gesture a subtle formal link to the beginning of the play, just as the exhausted triumvirate of Albany, Kent, and Edgar echoes Lear's original division of the kingdom. For as the first scene, with its talk of "all" and "nothing" on the part of Goneril, Regan, and Lear, presented us with towering absolutes, standards of affection and rejection that we knew to be false, as compared with the specificity, the sense of limit, in Cordelia's "no more nor less," so the last scene confronts us with the difference between life and death in terms of tiny particular distinctions we know to be truly absolute.

When Gielgud entered in this scene with Cordelia in his arms, his voice suddenly rose on the last word of "Howl, howl, howl, howl," and became a howl itself, an animal wail. He achieved here the kind of emotional renewal, the kind of continuing specificity lines of this type demand. He was taking advantage of the fact that the lines are at once a command and a cry. But they are unlike the commands Lear utters in the opening scenes because they *are* a cry, and because what they command is a sharing of feeling. Like so much in the play, they confront the performer, Lear's on stage audience, and the audience in the theater with the need to *keep* feeling, just when we might well wish to stop, to distance ourselves from the pain. And my point in this lecture has been that the role of Lear, as Shakespeare has written it, is designed to carry the audience forward into a deep exploration of its own relation to pain and to the problems of feeling and not feeling.

45

When Gloucester tells Lear that he has learned to see the world feelingly, Lear answers, "What! art mad?" For his own madness is a struggle in which he comes to acknowledge his feelings and through them to make a connection with the world that brings him instants of shared love and moments of illumination he could have attained no other way. But the play's ending makes certain that we do not sentimentalize these moments, that we continue to experience the kind of openness to feeling Lear achieves as something desperately difficult, charged always with a weight of possible terror. For to see feelingly means to introduce an element of risk into every human exchange, the risk of being incapacitated, driven mad, destroyed by what one feels. It is to remind oneself that one is always vulnerable, because one is not everything. "They lied when they told me I was everything," Lear says; and when Cordelia first tries to tell him that no one can be everything, his first reaction is to feel that she is nothing. But without that recognition of vulnerability, as the experience of the play reminds us, and as it must remind the actor who attempts the title role, without that constant focus on the dangerous human facts of feeling, we are nothing indeed.

Three

Shakespeare, the King's Company, and *King Lear*

G. E. Bentley

The great outpouring of books and articles on Shakespeare, on his plays and poems and characters and sources and his principles and his prejudices—this plethora is astonishing to the general public and terrifying to the scholar. A few days ago I had the temerity to look over the list of books and articles on Shakespeare and his works published in the single calendar year 1977. In this list there were 2,184 items, of a variety of types, but most of them were criticism, and I suspect that the same emphasis on criticism characterizes the complete bibliographies for a good many years before 1977. Let me begin, therefore, with some generalizations about Shakespeare criticism.

All too many of the critical discussions of the plays of Shakespeare derive from the critic's personal preconception of Shakespeare as a man. This basic preconception colors all the wise words of criticism that follow from it, but it is very unusual for these underlying assumptions to be openly stated. For most critics the assumption has probably become subconscious, or taken for granted. Critical articles in the 1960s and 1970s, for instance, do not begin: "I believe that Shakespeare was a subtle advocate of Women's Lib, ahead of his time. And for this reason in *King Lear* the armies of France are led by General Cordelia. And for the same reason the end of *The Taming of the Shrew* must necessarily be ironic." Books and articles displaying preconceptions such as these could be cited though they are really not very numerous. Far more common today is another preconception. If this popular preconception were openly stated it would read: "I believe that Shakespeare was, at heart, a scholar like me, working with his books in his study, and then, reluctantly, in order to feed the wife and kiddies, selling his masterpieces to those vulgar men the actors for performance in their crude theaters." If you have not perceived this self-flattering preconception grinning beneath the surface in many of the hundreds of Shakespeare articles that fill the learned journals and the critical reviews, then you have not read very many—yet.

Now such assumptions as these, from which numerous critics have taken off during the last two hundred years, tend to change from generation to generation. The preconceptions of the later twentieth century are not those of the eighteenth century, or of the nineteenth. During the reign of Queen Victoria a good many critics evidently conceived of Shakespeare as Alfred Lord Tennyson with a somewhat shorter beard. Obsessed with this conception many of them concluded that Shakespeare *could not* possibly have written what Tennyson *would not* have written. Therefore, in their numerous editions of the plays, they have cut out (or at least reduced to footnotes) most of those bawdy lines that Shakespeare and his audiences obviously enjoyed. This vulgar bawdiness (said the Victorians) must have been added to Shakespeare's pure lines by those nasty men, the actors.

But time passes on. In our own time the reverse attitude is often assumed. Every line in every play is examined for sexual allusions. And we have scores of sex-oriented articles written about the plays.

Our modern critics and the Victorian critics have read the same lines, but they began reading them with different preconceptions about the kind of man the playwright was. It is easy for us to see that he was not Alfred Lord Tennyson, but I wonder if it is as easy for us to perceive that he was not Sigmund Freud either. A great deal of Shakespeare criticism, alas, reveals to the reader more about the critic than it reveals about William Shakespeare.

These odd and earnest preconceptions of what sort of a man Shakespeare really was have been encouraged by the popular delusion that there exists very little documentary evidence about Shakespeare's life, and, therefore, we must recreate him from what we like to call our insights. Like many other popular beliefs, this one is totally false. A lot is known about the life of Shakespeare. Let me illustrate.

Playacting was fantastically popular in the period of the so-called Elizabethan drama. More than fifteen hundred plays of the period are known—at least by title. London had more theaters per capita than New York has today. More than two hundred and fifty writers are known to have tried their hands at English plays between 1585 and the closing of all theaters by law in 1642.

Among all these two hundred and fifty writers of plays, the ones whose lives are most fully documented are Ben Jonson and William Shakespeare. These numerous recorded facts may not be the ones the modern reader yearns to know, because the primitive seventeenth century had to do without licensed psychiatrists. But it is sheer perversity to ignore or to deny the many recorded facts in favor of one's own pet prejudices—Freudian or other.

The recorded facts show quite clearly what Shakespeare's major preoccupation was. It was the London professional theater. Very few men in his time—or in any time before or since—have been so completely involved with the theater in all its aspects as this man Shakespeare was.

First of all he was a professional actor, and in Elizabethan times that meant performing nearly every day when the theaters were allowed to be open and rehearsing most mornings. It was not uncommon for a professional troupe in the 1590s to perform fifty different plays in the course of a year. Throughout his London career Shakespeare was a member of a formally organized acting company, the most distinguished troupe of his time and, as far as I know, the most successful acting company in the history of the English theater.

In the year 1603, when King James I succeeded to Elizabeth's throne, the troupe of which Shakespeare was a leading member, that is, a patented sharer, was selected as the finest in the kingdom. It was granted a royal charter or patent to be the dramatic company of the king. This official charter, issued from the royal patent office, names the leading members of the troupe, William Shakespeare, Richard Burbage, John Heminges, Henry Condell, and five others. The same nine men were entitled to wear the king's royal livery. The first grant was made to Shakespeare and the others by the Royal Wardrobe when they were ordered to march in the coronation procession. As the royal company, the King's Men were made the same livery grant every second year until the royal establishment itself was broken up at the beginning of the great Civil War.

So far as the records still extant can tell us, the principal members of this company were Shakespeare's closest associates, remembered with fondness even after his retirement to Stratford. When he was on his deathbed in 1616, he made his last will and testament, disposing of a good deal of property. Most of the named legatees were Stratford relatives and neighbors. From his career of a quarter of a century in London he selected only three old friends for remembrance. All three were actors, all three were leading members of the king's company, all three were his associates in the ownership and operation of the Globe and Blackfriars theaters: Richard Burbage, John Heminges, and Henry Condell.

But Shakespeare was bound to his company not only as an actor, as a sharer in their profits, and as part owner of their two theaters. He had another most important connection with them. Years before he wrote *King Lear* for these players, Shakespeare had become the attached dramatist for the organization. Now what was an attached dramatist, or, as they were sometimes called at the time, poet-in-ordinary?

This position has been recognized and studied carefully only in the last few years.[1] Attached dramatists agreed to write

---

[1] See G. E. Bentley, *The Profession of Dramatist in Shakespeare's Time* (Princeton: Princeton Univ. Press, 1971).

exclusively for the troupe of players to which they were contracted. They agreed to provide a specified number of plays per year, usually two. They agreed to refrain from publishing any of these contracted plays without the consent of the acting company. The company could accept or reject any of the plays written for them. In most instances the attached dramatist seems to have had a weekly salary and a benefit performance. Generally the leading members of the company, that is, the sharers, sat together in a tavern to hear the play read before they accepted it for production.

London dramatic troupes bought many other comedies and tragedies besides those written specifically for them by their attached dramatist or poet-in-ordinary. As repertory companies they needed more new plays than the two, or sometimes three, provided for them each year by their attached dramatist.

The Elizabethan playwrights known to have been attached dramatists for at least part of their careers (and the number of plays they wrote) are Thomas Heywood (220); John Fletcher (69); Thomas Dekker (64); Philip Massinger (55); James Shirley (38); William Rowley (24); Richard Brome (23); and William Shakespeare (38). Shakespeare was not the most prolific writer in this group; he wrote about the average number of plays for a professional. Heywood, Fletcher, and Dekker wrote more than he did. But he was the playwright attached for the longest unbroken period to a single company. Of course he had one extra and special qualification—genius.

By the year 1605, when Shakespeare prepared *King Lear* for the royal company of King James, two-thirds of his plays had already been performed, all of them by this company or its lineal antecedents. The closeness of his relationship with the players of this troupe had been developed over fifteen years of constant teamwork in the theater. His intimacy with his company was as great as Molière's with his troupe at the Palais Royale; it was far longer than Henrik Ibsen's with the Christiana theater; it was much longer than Gilbert and Sullivan's association with the Savoy. So far as I can find, no playwright in the twentieth-century English or American theater has had as long or as close an association with a single company of players.

None of Shakespeare's plays is known to have been written for any other company. His plays were all written as part of his obligation to his company, and they were carefully fitted to the needs, the facilities, and the personnel of this troupe of players. When Shakespeare finished with his manuscript, it was no longer his property, but the property of the king's company of.which he was only a part. The company could act it, not act it, print it, or not print it as the sharers decided. Shakespeare never printed any of his comedies or tragedies himself.[2] Nor did he mention them in his will. This omission is not amazing, as it has seemed to mystery lovers who do not understand the workings of the Elizabethan theater. After Shakespeare had turned over his manuscript to the book holder of the king's company, it was no longer his property to bequeath. The play was the property of the acting company for which it had been designed and cast.

When finally the plays were all printed together in 1623, seven years after the dramatist was dead, the publication was with the consent and under the auspices of the king's company. This volume, now generally called the First Folio, has been revered for two centuries as one of the great treasures of literature. It has long been one of the items most sought for by great book collectors all over the world. The First Folio is indeed a treasure in both senses of the word. But it gives us more than the masterpieces of England's greatest literary genius: it is eloquent of his professional associations.

The First Folio was brought out by the business manager of the king's company, John Heminges, and his close friend, fellow sharer, and lifetime associate Henry Condell. For their book they wrote a preface about their "Friend & Fellow," as they call him, William Shakespeare. These two veterans of the king's company also published, as another piece of front matter for the First Folio, a list of players headed "The Names of the Principall Actors in all these Playes."

It has not often been noted just what this list of "Principall

---

[2] See G. E. Bentley, *Shakespeare and His Theatre* (Lincoln: Univ. of Nebraska Press, 1964), pp. 1-26.

Actors" really is. All these players had acted in Shakespeare's plays, but so had at least fifty other men and boys not named. Why did the editors select these twenty-six names only? It is not because they were the most recent actors, for several of those named by Heminges and Condell had been dead for years. It is not a list of the original actors of the company, for several of those named had not joined the king's company until after the author of the plays had retired from London and gone back to Stratford. As one might have expected in a collection of the plays of the official dramatist of the company edited by the official business manager of the king's company, it is an official list. Nearly all of these twenty-six men were patented members or sharers in the company.

In the context of our knowledge of Shakespeare as a man of the theater, a leading sharer in King James's dramatic company, a longtime associate of these players who had already acted in more than twenty of the plays he had written for them, and as their attached dramatist, what can we tell that he did when he began to write *King Lear* for his fellows in the year 1604 or 1605?

We know that he started with an old play, long since performed, based on a story written down in English about the year 1135, more than four hundred years before. The old Elizabethan play was called *The True Chronicle Historie of King Leir and His Three Daughters Gonerill, Ragan, and Cordella.* This method of beginning with a known story was normal in the theater of the time. The majority of the many hundreds of plays of the great Elizabethan outburst were based on stories that had already been printed as novels, histories, narrative poems, plays, or pamphlet accounts of contemporary events, usually crimes. This normal practice of the writers for the Elizabethan theaters was followed by the author of *King Lear* in most of his plays.

He began, then, with a rough outline of his story. He also began with another major advantage for any professional playwright looking toward production. Before he set pen to paper he knew all the actors who would be cast in the first performance of his new tragedy. Many of them he had known for a long time; his leading man he had known and worked with for at least thirteen years. Shakespeare had at his disposal ten major actors, including himself. These were his fellows (as they called each other), all of them official sharers in the enterprise of the king's company.

Besides these sharers he had, for the women's roles, several boys who were in training. At any given time not more than three or, sometimes, four of these boys had been through enough years of coaching to be trusted with substantial roles like Cordelia, Regan, and Goneril. In addition to these thirteen sharers and boy apprentices, the playwright had probably in 1604 about a dozen hired men, that is, minor actors and functionaries who worked for wages, not for shares in the profits. These hired men could be used for minor roles, such as Curan, or the Doctor, or the Herald, or the messengers. The influence of these casting facts is apparent in *King Lear*.

In his new play Shakespeare created twelve major roles. They are, in order of length:

1.	King Lear	765
2.	Edgar	397
3.	Kent	379
4.	Gloucester	344
5.	Edmund	323
6.	The Fool	253
7.	Goneril	196
8.	Regan	187
9.	Albany	156
10.	Cordelia	117
11.	Cornwall	110
12.	Oswald	80

In addition to these major figures there are about twenty-five smaller parts. But Shakespeare carefully arranged these minor roles so that each of the hired men could handle two or three different parts. For instance, the Duke of Burgundy appears only in act 1; the same actor could also have played

Curan in act 2 and one of Cordelia's soldiers in act 4. All of Shakespeare's plays, and most of those of his contemporaries, are planned for this kind of doubling. For instance, the forty-nine parts of *Julius Caesar* are skillfully managed so that they can be performed by sixteen actors, including hired men and boys.[3]

One of Shakespeare's problems as he was working out his scenario for *King Lear* seems most baffling to modern readers. He had to fashion all his female characters so that they could be performed at the Globe by boy actors. There were no women on the English stage when he was producing—nor for forty years after his death. All London dramatic companies in his time had boy actors in training, usually beginning about the age of ten. They were necessarily less experienced than the men. Usually they were finished as female impersonators by the age of fifteen or sixteen, when their voices changed, and new recruits had to be found. This difficult situation (which was perennial in dramatic troupes of the time) was once aptly described in a lawsuit in which the Burbages testified that "the boys [were] daily wearing out." The most experienced boy actors Shakespeare had to call upon in 1605 could not have had more than five or six years of training and experience in public appearances. In *King Lear*, as in his other plays, he was careful not to ask too much of his boy actors. In this play the leading adult actors—six of them—all have much longer roles than the boys. Lear, Edgar, Kent, Gloucester, Edmund, and the Fool all have bigger roles than Goneril, Regan, or Cordelia. Shakespeare has given to Richard Burbage as Lear six times as many lines as he has written into the role of Cordelia.

But however much Shakespeare was restricted in his development of Cordelia, Goneril, and Regan by the boy actor tradition, he had the great advantage of knowing just what these three boys could do well and what they did badly. He could develop the roles to suit the talents and the limitations

[3] William A. Ringler Jr., "The Number of Actors in Shakespeare's Early Plays," in *The Seventeenth Century Stage*, ed. G. E. Bentley (Chicago: Univ. of Chicago Press, 1968), pp. 110-134.

of his boys. Before he began to write, he knew which boys were best at creating bitches, like Goneril and Regan, and which one had done best in other plays as the honest, fearless and devoted girl. He never ran the danger that most modern dramatists have experienced and that we often see in our theaters: namely, an actress cast in a role that is not suited to her talents.

This close acquaintance and daily association of Shakespeare with the players who would create his roles in *King Lear* gave him even greater advantages when he was blocking out the major parts. His adult colleagues had been with him much longer than the boys had. He had had innumerable opportunities to observe the special talents and sad deficiencies of most of these players for whom he was creating roles in his new tragedy. Most familiar was Richard Burbage, who would be his Lear.

In the long years of their association Shakespeare must have watched Burbage on the stage hundreds of times—in performances at the old playhouse called the Theatre, at the new Globe, on the road during the company's many tours of the provinces, and in the company's many recorded command performances before Queen Elizabeth or King James at court. There are still extant official records of more than fifty royal shows presented at the royal palaces by this company in the years preceding Burbage's performance of *Lear* before King James at Whitehall Palace on Saint Stephen's Day in 1606.

How intricate and demanding was the role the dramatist prepared for his colleague Richard Burbage in this new play has been brilliantly analyzed by Professor Michael Goldman in his lecture. In the role of Lear the attached dramatist of the king's company asked from his friend and leading actor almost superhuman histrionic powers. Yet he knew what he was about. What he wrote for Richard Burbage in 1605 has continued to be the ultimate test for most of the greatest English-speaking actors. The role is such an actor's challenge that many players who are not English-speaking have had to attempt it in French or Italian or Russian or German. I wonder if Shakespeare ever thought that what Burbage could do, players of future generations could do?

Another actor whose talents and specialties influenced Shakespeare in the composition of *King Lear* was Robert Armin. His role was the Fool. Though this character does not appear in the first three scenes of the play and disappears before the end of act 3, he is vital for the effects in the great middle scenes of the tragedy.

It is noteworthy that comedians were important on the London stage in its greatest years. Usually these comedians were called clowns or fools; Shakespeare uses both names in his plays. Several of these comedians had great reputations in Elizabethan and Stuart England. The most famous ones like Tarleton, Kempe, Armin, Shank, and Cane are more frequently mentioned in contemporary references than the more serious actors, except Burbage and Alleyn. In song books and anecdotes and joke books and private letters and even in essays there are references to them and accounts of their practical jokes and impersonations and wisecracks. One of the earliest of these famous comedians was Richard Tarleton, who was selected as the nucleus for Queen Elizabeth's first royal troupe, formed in 1583. Clowns and fools were the darlings of the Elizabethan populace. Throughout the fifty-year history of Shakespeare's company, there were always one or two well-known comedians in the troupe.

Shakespeare composed roles for these professional funny men in the majority of his plays, in tragedies as well as histories and comedies. In his earlier plays he prepared roles for his fellow sharer, the famous clown Will Kempe—roles like Bottom in *A Midsummer Night's Dream*, Shallow in *Henry IV, Part 2*, Launcelot Gobbo in *The Merchant of Venice*, Peter in *Romeo and Juliet*, and Dogberry in *Much Ado About Nothing*. These roles, written for his plays in the 1590s, all have certain elements in common, but they are nothing like the Fool's part in *King Lear*. And one of the reasons for the radical change is Kempe's successor, the new comedian in the company for whom Shakespeare had to plan when he began to write his greatest tragedy. Armin was a man of some literary accomplishments. He had composed at least one play, called *The Two Merry Maids of Moreclack*. He wrote a book about the lives and exploits of several earlier comedians, called *Fool upon Fool; or, Six Sorts of Sots*. He had translated an Italian story and turned it into English verse. He wrote several prefaces for the books of other authors, including one preface for a religious book. John Davies wrote a poem to him as "honest gamesome Robert Armin."[4] Obviously Robert Armin was a man of divers talents. And he was the fellow actor of the king's company whom Shakespeare had in mind while he was shaping the role of the Fool in *King Lear*.

Armin most often played the type of professional fool, attached to a court, dressed in a long cloak of motley and a coxcomb. This type of fool appears in a number of the plays of the last half of Shakespeare's career after Kempe had left. The general type was familiar to the Globe audience not only from plays: the professional fool of King Henry VIII, Will Sommer, was still talked about and frequently referred to in the reigns of the first two Stuart kings. Many of the people in the audience at the Globe had seen the fool of James I, Archie Armstrong, about whom there are a number of stories.

The affectionate tolerance in which these court fools were held is conspicuous in Hamlet's address to the skull in act 5 of his play, in the graveyard scene. The gravedigger tells him that the skull that has just been thrown out is that of Yorick, the court fool of Hamlet's father, and Hamlet indulges in melancholy reminiscences that show the position of a court fool.

> Alas, poor Yorick! I knew him, Horatio, a fellow of infinite jest, of most excellent fancy. He hath borne me on his back a thousand times. . . . Here hung those lips that I have kissed I know not how oft. Where be your gibes now? Your gambols, your songs, your flashes of merriment that were wont to set the table on a roar?
>
> (5.1.183-191)

[4] Charles S. Felver, "Robert Armin, Shakespeare's Fool," *Kent State University Bulletin*, 49, no. 1 (1961):1-82; Leslie Hotson, *Shakespeare's Motley* (London: Hart-Davis, 1952), pp. 84-128.

This is the type of contemporary character Shakespeare asked Robert Armin to create in *King Lear*—the natural, held in affection and given extreme license at court, a license that irritated some people, as it does Goneril in act 1, scene 4, when she upbraids her old father with "This your *all-licensed* Fool."

This is the kind of character (found frequently in Elizabethan plays) that Shakespeare built up for Robert Armin. He dressed in the conventional costume of the court fool or jester, the long coat of motley and the coxcomb. Shakespeare makes Armin refer repeatedly to these articles of clothing. In his entrance speech Armin takes off his cap and hands it to Lear, saying, "Here's my coxcomb." He refers to this coxcomb four times in his next ten lines.

This leading comedian of the king's company for whom the part was prepared was also a well-known singer, and Shakespeare exploits his musical accomplishments in *King Lear*. Snatches of song are scattered through the part, and at one point he sings a whole stanza of the song "Heigh-ho, the wind and the rain" (3.2.75). Armin had sung this song before. When he had taken the part of Feste in *Twelfth Night*, Shakespeare had set him to sing all five stanzas of this song as a conclusion to the play. In modern performances of *Twelfth Night* it is instructive to note the telling effect of this conclusion when the comedian can really sing this melancholy song. Alas, modern comedians are seldom able to sing it well, and it is often cut out of modern performances of the play for the sake of the unmusical actor.

For *King Lear* Shakespeare has modified two lines of the song in order to enhance the pathos of its application to the mad Lear, but the repeated refrain is the same. Shakespeare had seen before what his fellow Robert Armin could do with this music, for instance, when his company had produced *Twelfth Night* in a private performance at the Middle Temple three years before. Shakespeare also had to shape the other characters in the play similarly—with the individual abilities of his fellows in mind. What did he do to fit a role to his old friend John Heminges? How was the new, rising actor in the company, John Lowin, handled in *King Lear?* And what happened when the dramatist read his new manuscript for the approval of his fellow sharers, probably in a private room in some tavern, perhaps the Mermaid? Did Burbage say in the middle of the reading of the third act: "Aw, come on, Will! You can't expect me to do that!" Did Robert Armin say at the end of the last act: "What the hell! Don't I come on in the last two acts at all?"

To such questions as these we shall never know the answers. My concern here is to plead that this is the context in which William Shakespeare must be imagined. He was no demigod sending down his precious manuscripts from Olympus, nor was he anticipating every future literary fad. He was a professional man of the theater, absorbed in the affairs of the king's company in all its ramifications.

And now you see *my* preconception of the kind of man William Shakespeare was. In the coming century future critics of Shakespeare's works may think that my preconception of this man of the theater is as deluded as the Victorian one. Or the Marxian one. Or the Freudian one.

Perhaps. But I don't really think they will.

Four

As the Wind Sits:
The Poetics of
King Lear

Theodore Weiss

Paradox, contradiction, extravagance, outrageous wit loom large among the ways we have of meeting life and Shakespeare at their ripest. And never is life more on the stretch than in *King Lear*. Blowing from all directions at once, a storm shapes into magnificent poetry that threatens to rip free of its moorings and to blast the play and its world to pieces. I will try to show that the storm, as it blows through the play's words, charging them with maximal power and grandeur, blows thing and thought apart and leaves those words madly flapping, tattered husks. Yet the play itself, storm and all, made of something like adamant, endures. How then exaggerate our problems with it, the mercuriality, the wonder, and the rigors we must contend with?

So I begin with an oxymoron as extreme as I can make it: *King Lear* is a monument of the stormiest music. For what help they may be, I recommend two additional paradoxes, the first formulated by the most balanced Greek tragedian, Sophocles: "Call no man happy until he is dead"; the second, by the modern poet most enthusiastic for the tragic spirit, Yeats, from his poem "Crazy Jane Talks to the Bishop," written in old age when he experienced some of the triumphant irascibility, the sexual ferocity, of Lear: "For nothing can be sole or whole / That has not been rent." Yeats pursued this in his "Lapis Lazuli" to an ultimate paradox in which he declared

Shakespeare's tragic heroes gay: "Gaiety transfiguring all that dread."

Armed with these observations, I mean to dare further extravagances, or what would certainly be extravagant for any work other than *King Lear*. A. C. Bradley, exercised like many other critics by the play's "inconsistencies," long ago plausibly compiled them. For me they confirm the play's plausibility. In fact, one might say that *King Lear*, taking on some of the materials of a *Titus Andronicus*, makes them necessary and convincing. But I would be sensible not to be too confident of my response except as I assume, at least as confidently, that it too is bound to be inadequate. Inadequate and, one might almost hope, extravagantly, egregiously, so perhaps germinally wrong. Already fifty years ago, in his "Shakespeare and the Stoicism of Seneca," Eliot suggested, "About any one so great as Shakespeare, it is probable that we can never be right; and if we can never be right, it is better that we should from time to time change our way of being wrong."

King Lear is extraordinary, to begin with, if only for the gamut of response, wrongness and all, it has elicited over its nearly four hundred years of survival. That gamut has gone from laudations of the play as the most sublime work of art ever produced to summary dismissals of it as a fiasco of childish absurdity. We must appeal to a major writer indeed for the best expression of the latter opinion. According to Tolstoy, *King Lear* prompts "aversion and weariness." But like a good, great competitor, Tolstoy never had a kind word for Shakespeare. Tolstoy's towering, stormy life and his dramatic runaway end, giving the lie to his contemptuous words, would seem to attest to the validity of *King Lear*. Even more awesome than Lear's surviving his daughters and his storm is his riding through the assault, favorable and hostile, of his host of critics, directors, actors—an assault revealing something fundamental about the play and also about the ages in which the critics lived as, squinting into its illuminating mirror, each found his own image.

Soon after Shakespeare's lifetime and during the Restoration, the play had little appeal. But in 1681, out of admiration,

Nahum Tate revived it, if with major alterations. As his Dedication says, "Nothing but . . . my Zeal for the Remains of *Shakespear* cou'd have wrought me to so bold an Undertaking." He fully recognized the uniqueness of Shakespeare's "Creating Fancy" and of the play's language and images, "the only Things in the World that ought to be said on those Conditions." Why then did Tate feel obliged to revise it? "I found the Whole . . . a Heap of Jewels, unstrung, and unpolisht; yet so dazling in their Disorder, that I soon perceiv'd I had seiz'd a Treasure." How apt is his description "dazling *in* their Disorder." But it is the unstrung and unpolished, jumbled-about condition of the jewels that obviously distressed him and his age. To make the play palatable for a Restoration audience, he gave it, among other things, a happy ending. As Boileau observed, "Some truths may be too strong to be believed." Or in Eliot's words from "Burnt Norton," "Human kind / Cannot bear very much reality." We are not far from Keats's "negative capability." Shakespeare's sources apart, he was after reality, reality as he knew it in all its relentlessness or, more accurately, in all its indifference, and not the conventions of any one time or society.

But a great change occurred in the nineteenth century. Charles Lamb well expressed the new attitude. Despising Tate's revision, Lamb felt the play "beyond all art" and Lear's "martyrdom" so complete that "a fair dismissal from the stage of life [was] the only decorous thing for him." Lamb was after the decorous and a fair dismissal, one from the stage itself. Like his fellow Romantics Lamb exulted in the sublime, in nature at its most extravagant. The very things about *King Lear* that repelled the eighteenth century delighted the nineteenth. But despite the play's horrors, its physical and other painfulness, or because of them, the Romantics seem to have wanted to exalt it out of existence; it was too good for this world.

Gradually the opinion of the play's inactability changed even though difficulties remained. Bradley, putting it beside works like *Prometheus Bound* and *The Divine Comedy*, calling it "Shakespeare's greatest achievement, but . . . not his best play," still considered it "too huge for the stage." Since then, however, the play has been generally applauded as great theater. We are too well rehearsed in horrors and hideous human behavior to boggle at *King Lear*. In some basic respects we may be closer to it than any age other than Shakespeare's own. And perhaps even closer than his own. Far flung through space as through time, fiercely questioning everything, we have proved outrageous in energy and ruin. But our present condition by that very ruinous energy has also destroyed the possibility of homogeneous response; and though the vast variety of our responses attests to the play's richness, it also attests to our confusion. Inevitably, in a time broken in its beliefs, a multiplicity of views accumulates.

Even so, whatever the time and however subtle and diverse the analyses, *King Lear*, like Lear himself, gaily fleeing, trailing wild flowers and a mad lilt of syllables, refuses to be caught. To land this light-as-air Leviathan, a critic would have to be able to throw out a net as large, as subtle, as complex as the play itself. Understandably critics now seize for dear life on one position or another, even one passage or verse, microscopically attended to, in the hope that it will be the clue to lead them through the tumultuous maze. At their best these concentrations illuminate moments of the play, as the Lilliputians, netting Gulliver, magnified his comb past any normal human capacity. But whatever light they may shed, the illuminations occur often at the expense of other parts and of the play as a whole, certainly of its furious speed, its battering unity; somehow it must be seen and heard all at once, a world experienced in the everywhere resonant round.

In attempting such a response, what immediately strikes me is the huge mélange of materials, a hurly-burly of them, filling the play. Set in a dark abysm of the past, the play seems porous as it lets loose countless fateful if invisible forces. Continuously, with one name or another, the characters strive to fix those forces. In and through these characters, most of all Lear himself, immensely heterogenous elements jostle one another. Like previous Shakespearean plays, *King Lear* is a veritable refuse heap: the wreckage of the ages, shadow-rich ruins, whispering in the wind. Odds and ends of folklore and sundry sources jut through: the Ur-*King Lear*, Sidney's *Arcadia*, Holinshed's *Chronicles*, Florio's translation of Montaigne, and other literary works, myths, cultural history, old songs. Many references, beyond being anachronistic, are thoroughly incongruous, like Edgar's medieval "Child Rowland" or the Fool's self-conscious, mind-jolting "This prophecy Merlin shall make; for I live before his time." Or Lear's calling Edgar a "learnèd Theban" and "good Athenian," as though Lear were an avid student of Plato and the other Greeks.

What a hodgepodge too of gods and supernatural powers is appealed to, from Hecate, Apollo, and Jupiter (rather odd deities, one might think, for ancient Britain); to natural powers, the orbs, the sun, moon, and stars; to nature itself, to Edgar's folk-superstitious fiends, borrowed appropriately from *A Declaration of Egregious Popish Impostures* since Edgar's Tom o' Bedlam is an imposture; to Lear's single God in "God's spies"; to his final gods throwing incense on him and Cordelia as "sacrifices." But, as Sidney and others had loudly complained, Elizabethan theater was always a gallimaufry. It splendidly presented the mind's baggage and often enacted its upheavals—a turmoil of terms and things, drawn higgledy-piggledly from countless times and places.

But this upheaval, further complicated by time's passing, is our basic dilemma: the staggering, if not impossible, effort required of us, first of all, to be accurate about the text itself, the play as it was in its own day. We must acknowledge our fundamental ignorance of that long gone day and the fact that its minds, whatever ambience they shared, were from one moment to the next variable. Second, we must recognize the congeries of buried cities, beyond the ones already there, the play became through the centuries—heaped Troys in ember state, ready, one or another of them, at any breath to flare up again. Finally, we must try to cope with the layer upon layer, in constant upheaval, of our own minds; for all times, as they seem to be in *King Lear*, are indeed contemporaneous in us, leaping at one moment to the nineteenth century, at another to the thirteenth, at the next to the Stone Age and earlier, the lot framed by modernity. All this while each age grapples with its special way of expressing not only its uniqueness but the inexpressible, and strives to capture in words what we always know is there precisely as it eludes us. Wallace Stevens, in his "Notes toward a Supreme Fiction," tells us that "Phoebus was / A name for something that never could be named."

But it is the extraordinary general uprootedness of these words or names in *King Lear*, their welter, that makes a difference and a difficulty even greater than that which we encounter in his other plays. From a not too sympathetic point of view, *King Lear* might be adjudged a ramshackle affair, a thrown-together contrivance that, worst of all, pieces flying, somehow holds together and works. Truly Nahum Tate's unstrung heap of jewels, "dazling in [if not for] their Disorder." So practiced was Shakespeare in the manipulation of diverse intellectual counters (he was fortunate to be born with his gifts when casual jumble was customary) that, by the time he wrote *King Lear*, he could make its miscellany serve, artistically, intellectually, emotionally, his darker purposes. His was, I suggest, an epical ambition to accommodate, as well as reality, the entire mind, its furnishings, its multiple deposits.

Furthermore, *King Lear* is what it is, one might speculate, because of Shakespeare's catch-as-catch-can style, his writing on the run. With an assignment of two, sometimes three, plays a year, he proved himself the genius of adaptability. Working under great pressure and at great speed, he was obliged to use whatever he could lay his hands on. Thus, to fill the play, he threw together the vastly miscellaneous material of his age and the materials lodged in his capacious mind. Writing at great speed, he had a heightened sense of, and could hold in his mind, the whole work at once. Little wonder it echoes and reechoes. He could hope to yoke, by his mind's incandescence and the violence of the play's situation, its immensely heterogeneous materials. Fortunately also, with models like Tamburlaine nearby, Shakespeare found a character, ancient, almost preternaturally powerful, able to confront that tumultuous everything (and nothing) and, with his rampageous spirit, able

66

to justify it if not to pull it all together into one meaningful harmony.

Now I propose that, helter-skelter as the United States has been from its start, a potpourri like *King Lear* is especially congenial to it. Already in the format of the journal, a grab bag of the whole of experience, Emerson and Thoreau were at their best. Can we deny this grab bag, all-inclusive characteristic to Whitman or to Melville in *Moby Dick*, obviously straining after Shakespeare? Moreover, the turbulence of the modern age, the art of Pound, Eliot, Joyce, Picasso, Stravinsky, and others, and our popular media have well developed our capacity for a *King Lear*. Anyone practiced in *The Cantos* or *The Waste Land*, in *Ulysses* and certainly *Finnegans Wake*, each a disgorging of the mind of the writer, a jamboree of materials looted from all times and places, should have a secure purchase on saltancies dizzying enough to require more than Puck-like, jet-propelled mental agility. These modern techniques are not merely a consequence or symptom of technology, the jumbled metropolis, the cheek-by-jowl surrealistic columns of the newspaper, the hither-and-yon of cinema, but a fairly accurate portrait of the feverish activity of the mind, especially of the liveliest examples of it in our time.

Yet, even as one stresses the potpourri aspect of *King Lear*, he may also observe how many things are missing from the play that we hardly think to miss. There is never a reference to Queen Lear or any other relative; nor is there one recollection out of Lear's more than eighty years and his surely tempestuous long reign that is not part of his obsession with his daughters' treatment. Further, beyond the necessary information that Edmund is a bastard (his mother, Gloucester's mistress, must be mentioned to establish Gloucester's character) and has been nine years out and must be nine to come, each time to some place unnamed, there is never a reference to a single memory in the Gloucester world. In short, whatever the remnants of allusions from earlier ages, fossils churned up in the characters' minds and speeches, only the here and now ferociously, overwhelmingly concerns them and us. One could rejoin, What do you expect? This is intensest drama. All such references, particularly domestic or historical ones, would be irrelevant, distracting, diluting. Nonetheless, though *King Lear* impresses us as being vaster than the other major tragedies, they are much richer in their recent past, its active presence.

At the same time *King Lear* is crowded with customs, conventions, and terms that rarely work—various gods, powers, fiends, religious and ethical concepts: kinship, love, marriage, friendship, the law of hospitality, a belief in the truth and its availability, kingship, hierarchy, nobility, the laws, and a plethora of things or objects, usually presented in speeches, hence, no more than words. Far beyond our cognizance, language in all of us is an amazing, mixed-up mosaic, the strata of time itself. But language in this play, more than that of other words, consists of haunting verbal relics from a world largely vanished: words, once possibly effective and satisfying, accepted as identical with reality and the gods, now dilapidated, having little to do with the actual lives of the characters. Ghostlike, the flicker of dead stars, these terms flit about in the wind. Though their sources have long withdrawn, they still hover near, and near perhaps mainly for Lear's and Gloucester's assumption, then Lear's relentless quest, of those sources as energetic realities.

Like its words the play's world itself is a plenitude out of strict economy, vastness and immense bustle out of emptiness; a stage almost as empty as the wind-swept moon encourages a bewilderment that hardly lets us know where, when, who, and what we are. Or in Lear's words, "Who is it can tell me who I am?" Where, beyond the castles of the main characters, never precisely located, does the play take place? In a wood; on a heath, another part of the heath, a hovel, a room in a suddenly present farmhouse somewhere near Gloucester's somewhere castle, and the one specifically named place, Dover, which is not Dover at all, with an altogether muffled battle in a field somewhere presumably near Dover (as later stage directions have it).

The play's landscapes crop up chiefly in speeches. Early on

the whole of Britain appropriately comes under Lear's official hands, but on a map and in most general terms, as he is about to tear Britain apart. Like a god, simultaneously creating a world and giving it away, as though it were his to give, he says to Goneril:

> Of all these bounds, even from this line to this,
> With shadowy forests, and with champains riched,
> With plenteous rivers, and wide-skirted meads,
> We make thee lady.
>
> (1.1.63-66)

And Regan's share?

> To thee and thine hereditary ever
> Remain this ample third of our fair kingdom,
> No less in space, validity, and pleasure
> Than that conferred on Goneril.
>
> (1.1.79-82)

Immediately, his land all gone, rather than crawling toward death, Lear rushes off to hunt. But where and what? Certainly, as far as we can tell, he returns with no spoils. Is it animals he is after, boars, dragons, chimerae, himself? Some brand new realm?

Beyond landscapes and animals, what people at large and their settings help to locate the play in time and place? None beyond Lear's "poor naked wretches" in the third act, in a passionate speech that instantly materializes such a wretch, Edgar feigning Tom o' Bedlam, a splendid anachronism straight out of Shakespeare's day and one of its worst horrors; then Edgar's "Bedlam beggars," never seen, like his never seen, somewhere "happy hollow of a tree" in which he hid from those hunting him, and his verbal "low farms, / Poor pelting villages, sheep-cotes, and mills. . . . "

And what is the play's single most striking scene? It is—like Lear's, words only and even less real than a map, if much more sensuously detailed—Edgar's magnificent, fantastic invention of the cliffs of Dover for the benefit of the blind Gloucester—truly pure poetry! Here, in an extravagant make-believe like his several roles, Edgar, as magically and effectively as Ariel with his storm and his masque, conjures up a vast vista in which he gives full play (though his other speeches, in tune with his roles, are also chockablock with a madly chaotic lot of creatures, times, phrases) to his imagination and composes a scene that by its contrast intensifies the bareness and the barrenness we have grown accustomed to in this play. Though supposed to be about the Dover cliffs, his speech is description without place, description as place, description uninfected, unembarrassed by actuality; thus it is free to fulfill its own gorgeous impulses and desperate needs. What we increasingly feel everywhere in *King Lear*, the tearing apart of words and the world, in this speech comes to complete, happy fruition.

Edgar develops a vision as clear and trenchant as a dream, by its very powerful absurdity all the more cogent and real. Edgar's "Lest my brain turn and the deficient sight / Topple down headlong" (4.6.23-24) gives the blind Gloucester his cue and his action. When Gloucester asks, "But have I fall'n, or no?" (4.6.56) Edgar, his imagination gaily free, as though he is urging his father to, instructing him in, the one wholly emancipating activity, that of the imagination, says, "Look up a-height; the shrill-gorged lark so far / Cannot be seen or heard: do but look up" (4.6.58-59). Words doubly effective for one blind! Edgar gives his imaginative powers an especial freedom when, at the moment's end, he describes the creature he pretended he had seen just before Gloucester's fall or his own pretended role on the summit:

> As I stood here below, methought his eyes
> Were two full moons; he had a thousand noses,
> Horns whelked and waved like the enridgèd sea. . . .

And then the explanation: "It was some fiend" (4.6.69-72). Gloucester, blind, in turmoil, is a perfect, credulous audience for such full-blown utterance. But this moment between Gloucester and his son, one of the several little plays within the play, no more and no less real than Lear's mock trial of his daughters, is what we expect of Shakespeare and what this whole play is: a world most telling in and out of words. Gloucester's incredible leap works as great poetry does, unerringly aimed at nothing but the mind's ear and eye, to their enlargement. Shakespeare had, in the nature of drama, practiced the verbal as reality from the start, but not till now with such audacity and thoroughness.

And the audacity increases the more we consider it. Beyond the storm, what season is it? What grows here? Wild flowers and weeds appear only in Lear's mad wearing of them, mainly in Cordelia's speech. Her description makes Gloucester's earlier words all the more striking:

> Alack, the night comes on, and the high winds
> Do sorely ruffle. For many miles about
> There's scarce a bush.
>
> (2.4.297-299)

So, too, critics have remarked, once Lear pulls up the staples of his world, an abundance of animals runs wild. But, as with Lear's hunting, other than in the speeches of the characters, in metaphor, where are they? The first we meet is, aptly, altogether fabulous and, aptly, out of Lear's rage—a dragon. The next is Gloucester's reference to Edgar: "He cannot be such a monster." Lear, wanting Oswald, exclaims, "How now? Where's that mongrel?" Horses are also frequently present in speech to be saddled somewhere and dashed off on; they image the frantic, helter-skelter quality of the play: "He calls to horse, and will I know not whither. . . ." Rage is especially imaginative at spawning the play's animals: Lear spews up "the sea-monster," "detested kite," "a serpent's tooth," a "wolfish visage." Or animals crowd forth for the measure of men and women. Edgar, claiming to have been a serving man, confesses he was "hog in sloth, fox in greediness, dog in madness, lion in prey." Later, Lear, trying those joint stools, his two daughters, says: "The little dogs and all, / Tray, Blanch, and Sweetheart—see, they bark at me" (3.6.61-62). Why should he not "see" these small, tame, pampered court dogs, see them turn on him, since he mistakenly "saw" his daughters in the first scene, now sees them, these lady braches, as the joint stools? With human creatures like these, "Tigers, not daughters," we scarcely need actual animals.

The condition of the elements and of the heavens in this play, again usually present through the main characters' speeches, also deserves attention. Lear, turning on Cordelia, swears

> by the sacred radiance of the sun,
> The mysteries of Hecate and the night,
> By all the operation of the orbs
> From whom we do exist and cease to be. . . .
> (1.1.109-112)

The language and the occasion achieve their solemnity through the series of genitives, which lends the passage an air of permanence and substance by establishing the major functions of heavenly bodies. (This, Lear's initial language of superauthority, will have to be broken.) Gloucester, a good-natured hedonist, seeks to attribute trouble, not to himself, but to external causes. He says,

> These late eclipses in the sun and moon portend no good to us. Though the wisdom of nature can reason it thus and thus, yet nature finds itself scourged by the sequent effects.
> (1.2.106-109)

Edmund, once alone, scoffs at this astrological notion as

> the excellent foppery of the world, that when we are sick in fortune, often the surfeits of our own behavior, we make guilty of our disasters the sun, the moon, and stars; as if we were villains on necessity; fools by heavenly compulsion. . . . An admirable evasion of whoremaster man, to lay his goatish disposition on the charge of a star.
> (1.2.121-131)

We can admire Edmund's vigorous good sense, his hardheaded understanding of weak human nature, even though he fails to see that he is a villain on necessity, one who has "chosen" to be what he is, a bastard, who therefore means to prosper outside the law and the conventions of society. But it is more important to recognize that, like Edmund, the villainous ones in the play, self-insulated, willful creatures, never acknowledge forces, larger than they are and mysterious, at work on them. Utterly practical, busy, rational beings, they are preoccupied with their own material desires, passions, plots. They live in one world only—this one—and have little use for images and imagining. They have successfully suppressed the dialogic, the other voice, in their natures. Only the good-natured in the play admit the existence of, even as they are also available to, mighty powers beyond themselves.

In many a previous Shakespearean play, upheavals in the weather, comets or furious storms, signalize an upheaval in the body politic, usually the deposing or the impending murder of a king; they imply the oneness of, or at least the intrinsic relationship between, man and nature. Gloucester, old-timer that he is, believes "these late eclipses in the sun and moon" ominous. And a great storm does blow up in *King Lear*, but not before or even during the deposing of a king. Instead it is the king himself, deposing himself, and the forces loose in the world that till then he had failed to notice, had been privileged enough to ignore or to think he controlled, that seem to release the storm. An overwhelming corrival presence rather than an omen, it buffets him and presumably those like him exposed, the poor and the mad, not the world he has been plucked out of or those responsible for his expulsion.

Shakespeare's first plays reveal his fondness for storms; and this fondness throughout his career deepened and expanded their significance far beyond their local dramatic effectiveness till a tempest becomes the principal figure or at least the title, initial setting, and impetus of his last play. Frequently these storms in the chaos they produce challenge the authority of a king. Can he, the absolute sovereign of his state, subdue the raging elements, make them, like his subjects, civil? Or is he, like King Alonso in *The Tempest*, powerless before them? It is important and amusing to remember that in that play, through his artistic magic, which controls the very air, another ruler, one deposed mainly because of his absorption in matters other than ruling, is responsible for rousing this tempest, or at least the illusion of it—a splendid, convincing bit of theatrics, on the order of Edgar's staging and then dispelling of the cliffs of Dover. In *King Lear* a deposed ruler also seems consonant with a storm; but, unlike magical Prospero, as he has no Ariel to make it, so he has no Ariel to curb it.

Lear's magniloquence from the outset, common to Shakespeare and his time, prepares us for Lear's outpourings in the storm. His sky-assaulting speech, something like his normal element, makes Lear and the storm a thunderous duet, two mouths with one air, each inspiring the other. Here Lear's speech goes so far that it tries the very limits of utterance. At first it is almost wholly externalized, that of a dragon or a grandiose man of stone. But forced inward, Lear grows more and more resilient and various in his speech. At last Shakespeare asks all and more of his own seemingly inexhaustible poetic resources by seeking out occasions so extreme that even his eloquence falters and thereby is most telling in such simplicities as Othello's "O!O!O!" and Lear's many-times-repeated "nothing" and "never." But the passions in Shakespeare's work, as in his world, are much more fully expressed than with us. They do seem close to nature in its wildest outbursts. Shaw could say of Othello's words that they are "streaming insignia and tossing branches to make the tempest of passion visible." King Lear's language, echoing the storm, appears to fan it into greater force. By the fiery verbal breaths these figures take they seem to draw the sky, the heavenly bodies, the very cosmos into their orbit.

In recent times, with emphasis on that resonant language, out of our preoccupation with the lyrical and, therefore, with the text itself, we have had the benefit of frequent studies concentrating on individual words and phrases. Caroline Spurgeon and then the New Critics brought resoundingly home to us the astounding echo chamber that is a Shakespearean tragedy. Spurgeon tells us that "only one overpowering and dominating continuous image" pervades *King Lear*, namely, the general 'floating' image kept constantly before us, chiefly by means of the verbs used, but also in metaphor, of a human body in anguished movement, tugged, wrenched, beaten, pierced, stung, scourged, dislocated, flayed, gashed, scalded, tortured and finally broken on the rack.

No wonder Lamb shrank from the play's visualizing or Tolstoy felt "aversion and weariness." "All through the play," Spurgeon continues, "the simplest abstract things are described in similar terms"—that is, violent ones. With the kingdom, the beloved sacred earth, broken by Lear's first act and with his curses and their consequences, wrenching chaos must follow, chiefly in the frenzied thoughts and speeches of the principal characters. Moreover, how can characters so sealed off, none more so than Lear himself, reach out of their emptiness and solitude, their vast empty world, toward each other except through violent deeds and stormy, violating words? Violence and the nothing its destructiveness must produce constitute their principal unity, their almost exclusive community.

The word "nothing" itself, sounded at the first, reverberates throughout the play. Lear, increasingly aware that he is not "everything," is thereafter on the hunt for "something," especially the "something else." Driven by his passionate need to understand the nature of things, to ferret out the truth, he hurtles round. But he does not find it till he sounds "nothing" through and through. Another word, "nature," and its variants, "natural," "unnatural," and "denatured," repeated with hammering insistence at least forty-seven times, accumulates immense significance. The nature of nature, human and otherwise, is crucial to the play. Additional recurrent words, "cause," "serve" and "service," "authority," "patience," "folly," once uttered, also hang in the air, waiting to be recalled. Words are, as I have proposed, the potent ghosts of the play.

Whatever diverse sides and diverse levels of meaning they reveal, these words, live staples, establish among them a delicate yet tensile network along whose taut lines the play and we live. Charged to begin with, enriched in new contexts, they become their own and the play's memory and energy. Every word, in a sense a key to the whole, acting as the play's center, in its moment of utterance bears the play's entire weight. It is almost the only work I know in which words, achieving their maximal pitch of resonance as of meaning, seem to be listening as they speak, fulfilling the Old Testament prophet's prediction of a time when each word will be simultaneously a tongue and an ear. Almost by their very ghostliness they become things in themselves. *King Lear* is that most contradictory thing, a drama of epical power, composed, prose and all, like a delicate lyric. Here terror, the abyss, nothing grow substantial with the abrupt shifts, the vaguenesses, the nuances of a symbolist poem. Most terrifying because of the vagueness. Dread and awe, usually out of myth, gods, monsters, become even more awful in *King Lear* for the gods' and monsters' murmurous, omnipresent absence.

The play opens, cheerfully and ironically, in prose and in a low key with the commonplace, life as it normally is. Fundamentally attractive, practical characters, Kent and Gloucester, accurately reflect the mundane human condition. Thus the scene begins, in medias res, with a casual mental error, a fallacious assumption, that sets the nature of the play. Kent says, "I thought the King had more affected the Duke of Albany than Cornwall." (Both Lear and Gloucester will proceed, on the basis of this assumption, to their dooms.) Kent assumes, therefore, that Lear will give more of the kingdom to Albany. But despite Lear's desire to be impartial, he will soon succumb to the favoritism Kent takes for granted in him. Then, before his bastard son, Gloucester makes much of his adultery, already something outside the laws of their society. It is the jocosity of Gloucester, his devil-may-care attitude, before his own wrongdoing that reveals to us the nature of the world we are about to enter, its arrogance, its selfishness, the cruelties arising from its selfishness, and the outrages they must spawn. It does not occur to Gloucester, talking about Edmund in the third person yet affectionately, to consider his son's feelings. Perhaps, since he is a natural child, Gloucester assumes that Edmund accepts such talk as natural. Edmund's first vivacious soliloquy, apostrophizing nature as his goddess, suggests that he does. For his own satisfaction he will, following Gloucester's example, surpass his father's conduct.

In the next scene, the royal auction, matters are reversed. Here official poetry prevails, as far from the first scene's speech as possible. It has nothing to do with daily reality or things as they are. We see at once the two kinds of life that are going on, one, the daily, about to invade and take over the other, the mythical. We had learned from Gloucester that the division of the kingdom had already been settled. This scene is little more than a playlet by Lear, his last official act, his most extreme, to fulfill, he says more profoundly and prophetically than he can know, his "darker purpose." Still he is entirely serious. He at least, if not the others, believes in the ceremony. Imperious, he is full of the pomp and sway of his office at the moment of surrendering it. Yet Lear and Gloucester meet in their unwitting callousness. For what Lear is after is the pleasure of hearing his daughters vie in public for his affection. He expects them to "perform." And he is conducting a bartering contest: the strongest bidder will win the largest prize. Words are to be taken at their face value. The play from the start then is a matter of calculation. The dominating elders set the code: values of love and feeling can, they think, be weighed and equated with property. Gloucester admits that lawful Edgar is "no *dearer* in my *account*." Yet though he says Edmund "the whoreson must be acknowledged," the acknowledgment seems to come to little more than that Edmund "hath been out nine years, and away he shall again." Lear, even as he equates himself with his kingdom, in his distribution of the kingdom blatantly equates love with land or property. How shall Edmund and Goneril and Regan not be the triumphant products of this attitude? In the same way, adultery, set by the first scene, grows into a central focus of the play, into Lear's furious disgust with sex, the source of life, as the poisoning of life.

This court scene has been called (or been accused of being)

a fairy-tale moment. In a deep sense it is, till reality breaks in. The play starts, far more than Lear can realize, at a climax where most plays end. It presents Lear, a veritable Titan, high above the others. He, among the clouds, is about to do what no other mortal can do or at least has the right to do. Having dealt fully with younger kings like Richard II, their being deposed and the havoc that ensues, Shakespeare now undertakes a harder task: depicting an aged king voluntarily about to depose himself and in the act, even as he hopes to establish peace and a tranquil conclusion for the end of his life, speeding anarchy. Richard II, also accustomed to living exclusively in his own highfalutin language as reality, insisted that only he could depose himself; and he also put on a superb spectacle in the act. But however eagerly he rushed to his splendid new role, he soon lost not only the crown but also his life.

At his advanced age Lear would seem, in his first act, to have reached his pinnacle and the end. Most daringly Shakespeare makes him go higher by a plummeting down. For grandeur and natural strength like Lear's this act has to involve a desperate plunge, especially impressive beside Gloucester's pseudoleap. Gloucester believes suicide devoutly to be wished. Lear, never given to such weak thoughts as this, must experience a long, fiercely dramatic day of exuberant dying, a head-on collision with all the elements of doubt and denial. He must be tried, his every inch of king, by pain, by the extremest suffering, that, finally, his kingliness be proved. His inveterate self-deception, the obduracy of it, requires that seemingly endless protraction of his ordeal.

The fairy-tale quality of the first Lear scene brilliantly reflects his condition. For many years he has been able to live in a fictitious world, near his heart's desire. Like Richard, who can hardly think himself anything other than king, Lear assumes his will the will of nature, identical with justice and the gods. Whatever his past conduct, given his personal power, in this respect different from Richard's, one might consider him a Richard who has managed to stay alive. Now, as Lear himself sees, the time has come for him to divest himself of the burden of kingship to "crawl toward death." He expects to relieve himself of kingship's cares but to retain, taking it for granted as his inevitable right, "the name, and all th' addition to a king." It never occurs to him that, with "The sway, / Revènue, execution of the rest," the title and its honors also go, that the name, a mere word, is meaningful only with the sway.

Never balked before, now piqued as a king and a father, Lear is outrageous to Cordelia. He is astonished by her response, ashamed, offended in public and, worst of all, at the moment of what he regards as his most generous deed. Had he not been justified to assume that Cordelia, his dearest love, would be eager to declare her love? Kent, a kind of son to Lear, crossing him immediately after (the second instance of challenge), makes the moment worse. It is as though those Lear most counted on have proved least trustworthy. By the momentum of the ceremony itself Lear is obliged to go on; once started, nothing can stop it. The king of him must suppress the father in him, something not hard to do since that father is also deeply hurt. Here at last Shakespeare's long line of testy old fathers, their wills frustrated by their daughters, but usually little more than bit parts, comes to a climax; the role steps forward to command the center of the stage.

At the outset we find Lear forbidding, even repellent, in the wanton indulgence of his rage. But we are soon drawn into his eruptive passion. If we at first fear him for his age, since it predicts our own and seems destructively infectious, we soon are awed by the strength of his feelings and by his endurance. In fact, we take heart and reassurance from him. Yet terror and pity also thrive in our response—terror that so much can still happen to an ancient king who, living long in a terrestrial paradise, seemed impervious to the trials of the rest of us, and pity that such suffering can be extracted from him. Yet, in the very horror Lear undergoes, Shakespeare shows that hope exists for us all till the day we die. Altogether indurated to being king, Lear must submit to the terrible wrenching that tears him from that role, from the stony shell it has become.

Thrust out of his world, the thinness and fakery of which

he is quickly obliged to see, he is exposed to naked nature and, stripped bit by bit, to his own naked human nature or, finally, as no appeal, no term works, to nothing. When the human world that is built, whatever its artificialities and pretenses, on and out of nature collapses, chaos bursts forth. Lear, a king supposed to establish and maintain order, having released the forces that destroy it, must seek out the center of that chaos, grapple with it to the death. He has the nobility to do so. At the same time he must discover the chaos and the madness of the human world, the savagery lurking under words, manners, clothes. "Nothing," obedient to his early command, comes between this dragon and his wrath; in his own person he must experience all that wrath to discover what treasure, if any, lies buried within and around him.

The loneliness he encounters he now realizes is what he by his insulated kingship has always been immured in. But fortunately his loneliness, oppressive as it is, is not complete. Though we see how long it takes before Lear notices and actually talks with others, he is, pitifully it would seem, companioned by his Fool, a shadow of a man. Yet the Fool in his love for Lear proves efficacious, a guide and teacher, perhaps as that felicitous old ne'er-do-well Falstaff was for Hal. A natural and, as we say, touched, the Fool, aside from being deeply touched by Lear's predicament, is in touch with forces most of us, locked away in our sanity, never know. Earlier times believed naturals sacred, possessed of preternatural powers, yet therefore to be feared, if not shunned. By his broken wits the Fool is out in the open. He has let the world in and to a considerable degree is capable of equaling the hodgepodge I earlier remarked, of seeing things as they are. Like his condition, the Fool introduces into the play a medley of styles, many-sided suddennesses Lear must learn: adages, charms, riddles, songs, obscenity, Mother Goose applied, snatches of nonsense, even a kind of surrealism, and the earthy wisdom that adheres to them.

The fool, the natural, in Lear must be released. If he can not be sole or whole in being rent, at least he must experience all the tatters. Gradually Lear, who has carried on monologues and at best delivered one-way orders to others, overhears, hears, then responds directly. He too is at last in touch. Only Hamlet has anticipated something like the Fool's piercing "madness," the freedom of insight it affords. Falstaff, also outside the confines of society, shares the Fool's rare common sense, his grasp of reality, and his wit, his drollery, his playfulness. Whatever their prudentiality, both see through the world's follies. Though beyond the play's generally oppressive atmosphere there are no ghosts, no witches (Lear does call his two daughters "unnatural hags"), no supernatural beings in *King Lear*, which would seem to invite them at least as much as any other Shakespearean tragedy, the Fool serves his play in a similar capacity as far as his person allows. For the very thing, his being a natural, that enriches the Fool also deprives him. He is wise enough to see the desperateness of his state. "I had rather be any kind o' thing than a fool." Any kind, that is, other than the witless Lear: "thou hast pared thy wits o' both sides and left nothing i' th' middle." Yet, so we have heard, nothing can be sole or whole that has not been rent.

Usually full of songs, the Fool is fuller than ever in his grief, his pining away at Cordelia's banishment and at Lear's as well. To Lear's "When were you wont to be so full of songs, sirrah?" the Fool replies:

> I have used it, nuncle, e'er since thou mad'st thy daughters thy mothers; for when thou gav'st them the rod, and put'st down thine own breeches,
> [*Singing.*]
> > Then they for sudden joy did weep,
> > And I for sorrow sung,
> > That such a king should play bo-peep
> > And go the fools among.
> > > (1.4.173-179)

Lear, his grief intensifying his awareness, adopts the Fool's language and something of his demeanor. Inspired by him and then by Edgar as Tom o' Bedlam, Lear emerges as a new kind of king, "crowned" with weeds and wild flowers, "As mad as the vexed sea; singing aloud" (4.4.2) and gamboling about. Close to nature, the freedom of undifferentiated "nothing," Lear has become, after Edgar, a Tom o' Bedlam (it is as though, in his newly sympathetic person, he has taken all beggars into his being), coupled with a Green Man, a Jack-a-Green, and gay; gaiety transfiguring all that dread. Perhaps another term needs to be added to tragedy's classical pair, terror and pity, namely, exultancy. And this play has it, tragical mirth, the violent mixture of emotions, one needed to express the other in its extremity, like Dante's Arnaut Daniel, singing as he weeps, weeping as he sings, groaning as he grows, growing as he groans. So this play is a mighty song out of grief, a jubilant acknowledgment, if not celebration, of our frailty, helplessness, anguish. This much we have as a way, our chief way perhaps, of meeting "the desolation of reality."

Gloucester and Cordelia will also know a mixing of the extremes of feeling. Again we meet an instance of the jostle of elements *King Lear* excels in. Cordelia's emotion is described to Kent by a gentleman who had delivered letters to her on her father's predicament:

> You have seen
> Sunshine and rain at once: her smiles and tears
> Were like a better way: those happy smilets
> That played on her ripe lip seemed not to know
> What guests were in her eyes, which parted thence
> As pearls from diamonds dropped. In brief,
> Sorrow would be a rarity most belovèd,
> If all could so become it.
>
> (4.3.19-26)

Edgar tells of his father's last moment when Edgar at last revealed his identity.

> But his flawed heart—
> Alack, too weak the conflict to support—
> 'Twixt two extremes of passion, joy and grief,
> Burst smilingly.
>
> (5.3.198-201)

Cordelia and Edgar assume the Fool's function once he reaches his limits. Edgar the "Athenian," in some sense Lear's noble "pagan" guide through the worst portion of human hell, and Cordelia, not "a soul in bliss" but a blessed creature, his guide through his purgatory, serve Lear as he becomes available to them. We can see why Tate and others for one hundred and fifty years insisted on arranging their marriage. Edgar, like many of the characters in the comedies, disguised to preserve themselves against an alien world, or fleeing their society to hide in the woods, assumes "the basest and most poorest shape / That ever penury, in contempt of man, / Brought near to beast" (2.3.7-9). He almost envies the poor Tom o' Bedlam he is playing, for little as Tom may be, "That's something yet: Edgar I nothing am" (2.3.21). Play, even as desperate as this, beyond their exigencies a product of their lovely, surplus energies, fulfills Shakespeare's best characters. Edgar has the imagination to play out such a desperate role and, in his quiet, observant youth, imagination enough to learn from it. If *King Lear* has an overseer and commentator, it is he.

The pinnacle of Shakespeare's art is reached when the mad Lear with his semimad Fool engages this feigning madman; together they sing a supreme trio. The vast heath seems empty except for the storm and these forlorn few, refugees, bare survivors, who clutch each other. At Lear's asking "What hast thou been?" Edgar promptly images an additional role for himself, a life crammed with sinful memories.

> A servingman, proud in heart and mind; that curled my hair, wore gloves in my cap; served the lust of my mistress' heart, and did the act of darkness with her; swore as many oaths as I spake words, and broke them in the sweet face of heaven. One that slept in the contriving of lust, and waked to do it. Wine loved I deeply, dice dearly; and in woman out-paramoured the Turk.
>
> (3.4.84-91)

Lear, who will recall Edgar's description of immorality and

improve on it, responds to Edgar's physical condition and to his naked confession:

> Thou wert better in a grave than to answer with thy uncovered body this extremity of the skies. Is man no more than this? . . . Ha! here's three on's are sophisticated. Thou art the thing itself; unaccommodated man is no more but such a poor, bare, forked animal as thou art. Off, off you lendings! Come, unbutton here.
>
> (3.4.100-108)

At last we have man, the thing itself, without any comforts or cushionings, without religion, philosophy, society. The Fool, turning to thoughts of sex this undressing suggests, remonstrates with Lear:

> Prithee, nuncle, be contented, 'tis a naughty night to swim in. Now a little fire in a wild field were like an old lecher's heart—a small spark, all the rest on's body, cold. Look, here comes a walking fire.
>
> (3.4.109-112)

Patly on cue appears the old lecher Gloucester with a torch. Later blind Gloucester and mad Lear, confronting each other, catapult us to a comparable height.

By now this jumble that the storm has produced is at its best, appositely in Lear's mad speeches. His sudden leaps from the mighty and all-powerful to the most minute, the least significant—a lap dog, a wren, a mouse, a fly—are part and parcel of the jostle of elements I have emphasized. These leaps are also a unifying, electric current in the world of the play and a mark of the agile, complete desperation of Lear's mind. To such frenzy an attempt at comprehending, at all-encompassing must come! We have in his words a veritable geyser of things and creatures that the ultimate storm would deliver itself of. Or, in Lamb's words, "the explosions . . . terrible as a volcano . . . turning up and disclosing to the bottom that sea, his mind, with all its vast riches." In *King Lear* the chain of being has indeed been broken, but the links of that cosmic bracelet are still present, dazzling in their disorder as they ricochet off one another.

For moments like those on the heath one must go to the Book of Job or *Don Quixote*. Job would have understood images like Lear's

> Nor rain, wind, thunder, fire are my daughters.
> I tax not you, you elements, with unkindness.
> I never gave you kingdom, called you children. . . .
> . . . .
>
> But yet I call you servile ministers,
> That will with two pernicious daughters join
> Your high-engendered battles 'gainst a head
> So old and white as this.
>
> (3.2.15-24)

Job's situation is even more extreme than Lear's. Despite his virtue, he is stripped, like Lear, first of his wealth, then of his children, and assailed in his own person. His friends insist his sufferings must prove his guilt. Job spurns them. And at last, by a tenacity and outcries like Lear's, he summons forth the Whirlwind. Agreeing to debate with him, It first requires his knowledge of the universe: "Where were you when the world was made, the stars, the animals?" The Voice in the Whirlwind parades the latter in all their splendor before Job. Beaten into new awareness, awed by the mightiness of the bewildering plenitude of creation itself, he realizes how petty, if not irrelevant, his questions and doubts are.

King Lear also puts all into question. Like Job, Lear is sorely tried to rouse this questioning in him. But Lear's day is much later; and though his storm is immense, and as searching in its way as is Job's, it never becomes a voice in dialogue with Lear beyond the harmony of storms I suggested earlier and the myriad voices that break out of Lear's battered self. As with Job, whatever realization Lear achieves, it is expressed, not in things or possessions, but, as he is broken open to a larger world and its creatures, in an expansion of himself, a participating in others beyond that self. At last he too learns, far past the prudent sense of the Fool's homely adage, to sit as the wind sits and to make "use of nothing." The Fool puts it clearly enough:

> He that has and a little tiny wit,
>> With heigh-ho, the wind and the rain,
> Must make content with his fortunes fit,
> Though the rain it raineth every day.
>> (3.2.74-77)

And Lear replies, "True, my good boy." While force is on our side, it is delectable. But once it cannot make use of us, it tosses us aside. Then patience or resignation seems our only resort. The spectacular tragedy here derives from Lear's endurance and resistance, both so mighty that they summon forth ultimate force or violence.

At the end, when he seems shattered, it is the touch and loving presence of Cordelia that restores him, along with the repose and the music the Doctor, as always in Shakespeare, prescribes—music, that opposite of the tempest in man and out, that imaging of order, its model the comportment of the spheres "from whom," Lear long ago declared, "we do exist and cease to be." Ears not tuned in, like eyes without feeling, or light without warmth, must prove inadequate. Feeling and thought, sight and insight are, briefly at least, brought together in Lear. For me Shakespeare is saying that, till the day we die, we may be realized. It is, sardonically, Lear's folly, his assumption of absolute authority, that lets the forces loose to try him, and so to bring him to his senses and authentic royalty. Truly acting as his mothers, his daughters give him belated birth and the exposure needed to mature him. Kent, waiting in the stocks for daybreak, can say, "Nothing almost sees miracles / But misery" (2.2.168-169). And Lear arrives at a similar sentiment even more extremely: "The art of our necessities is strange, / That can make vile things precious" (3.2.70-71).

This exploration of our astounding capacity constitutes the positive side of the play, its exhilaration, its tragic joy. Also part of this side is its unblinking expression, the affirmativeness that is the play's poetic language, that these things can exist and can be seen and said intensely, precisely, delicately. Positive, too, is Shakespeare's expectation of, his respect for, us, his audience, and our capacity to undergo all the trials of the play. Like Job, Lear experiences the universe at a depth and a height that sweeps away all lesser considerations. "What is the cause of thunder?" (3.4.153) Lear asks, realizing "the thunder would not peace at my bidding" (4.6.101-102). (But it does teach him the truth not only about himself, as he progresses from assuming he was everything to realizing he is one among many, then only a tiny part of the whole, and, finally, nothing, but also about his deceitful daughters: "there I found 'em, there I smelt 'em out.") Much later in another context Cordelia replies, "No cause, no cause." Thunder is resounding cause enough, an answer and an end in itself, as inexplicable and undeniable in its way as Cordelia's irrevocable love for Lear, as irrevocable as her gentle, yet self-possessed loveliness.

No longer believing in easy causality or in the rewards that are guaranteed the good, we must see feeling and goodness as their own rewards, or see nothing. It is how we experience our lives that matters. And when the appetite for whatever happens is courageous and ambitious, even attendant loss becomes a kind of advantage, if not a prize. Shakespeare, at the threshold of the modern world, in *Hamlet* and *King Lear* provides the boldest, most searching examination of that world's fundamental dilemma: the falling apart of thing and thought, thought and feeling. That Shakespeare should situate that dissociation in mythical Britain! But did it not take place in that first place, Eden? What is that outcast man's place— has he any—in the universe? And how, given that universe's composition, establish such a place? The inconsistencies, the mishmash of materials and attitudes, the multilayered, past-echoing present are what Shakespeare is proposing here— what, on this midden of a star, still hot, still eruptive, our world is made of: rocks, tempests, creatures, corpses, ideas in the word-laden air. Each of its own time and place yet jostling one another, they converge on our here and now. This convergence and the storm it releases, the headlong storm of Shakespeare's mastery, supply the play's overpowering unity, its tumultuously driven singleness.

Near the end Lear looks to the peace of a prison for Cordelia and himself. That he should think it the "nursery" he originally sought! Is he not as deluded as ever? For the naive ambition and illusion (one present in Shakespeare's earliest plays) of withdrawal from this world, out of the path of the winds of fortune, never succeeds:

> Come, let's away to prison:
> We two alone will sing like birds i' th' cage:
> When thou dost ask me blessing, I'll kneel down
> And ask of thee forgiveness: so we'll live,
> And pray, and sing, and tell old tales, and laugh
> At gilded butterflies, and hear poor rogues
> Talk of court news; and we'll talk with them too,
> Who loses and who wins, who's in, who's out;
> And take upon's the mystery of things,
> As if we were God's spies: and we'll wear out,
> In a walled prison, packs and sects of great ones
> That ebb and flow by th' moon.
>
> (5.3.8-19)

(The last image seems to have borrowed something from Falstaff. Yet the attitude, with its old tales and laughter, may be closer to Falstaff's than one at first realizes.) We recall Richard II, also in his final prison, attempting to make a world out of his imagination and his bare surroundings, but failing before the death he meets heroically.

Lear, finally, a mighty king once more, every raging inch of him, his last strength upon him, the fierce humanness he has never wholly surrendered, having killed Cordelia's executioner, enters with her in his arms for his last scene; far more awing it is than the first. But now he is a giant howl against the onlooking "men of stone" of whom he once was a prime example. He mourns the intolerable, ungainsayable fact of Cordelia's death: "She's gone for ever. / I know when one is dead and when one lives; / She's dead as earth." But instantly he shies away from this certainty: "Lend me a looking-glass [borrowed, one might say, from Richard II]; / If that her breath will mist or stain the stone, / Why, then she lives." Then he resorts to a feather, which he thinks stirs. Suddenly, proving how little we can be sure even of death and of our own senses, even as he says "she's gone for ever," he believes out of the strength of his desire that he hears her:

> Ha,
> What is 't thou say'st? Her voice was ever soft,
> Gentle and low, an excellent thing in woman.
>> (5.3.273-275)

Instantly he follows her gentleness with the ferocity of "I killed the slave that was a-hanging thee." Capping irony this is, for it was this voice of the one dearest to him, a voice so soft and low he failed to hear its true sentiments, that set him off on his disastrous course.

But, starting up again and for the last time, he exclaims at her irreparable death:

> And my poor fool is hanged: no, no, no life?
> Why should a dog, a horse, a rat, have life,
> And thou no breath at all? Thou'lt come no more,
> Never, never, never, never, never.
>> (5.3.307-310)

Just as he had, in the middle of the play, unbuttoned before the beggarly, seminaked Edgar, now before the dead Cordelia he says in heartbreaking simplicity that looks to the final nakedness, "Pray you, undo this button. Thank you, sir." From so little we and the world hang. In the end, by her reticence, Cordelia deceives Lear still. And still to the end he fails the truth. For even as he dies he cries out, "Do you see this? Look on her. Look, her lips, / Look there, look there." However we interpret these words, he has finally found satisfaction. "Call no man happy until he is dead." Such struggle, such suffering out of searching and searching because of suffering, perhaps our liveliest moment, may be our only way, at least briefly, of breaching worlds, holding them together.

The last words properly belong to Kent, "The wonder is he hath endured so long: / He but usurped his life." And to Edgar,

> The weight of this sad time we must obey,
> Speak what we feel, not what we ought to say.
> The oldest hath borne most: we that are young
> Shall never see so much, nor live so long.
>
> (5.3.325-328)

Kent's "wonder" is happily ambiguous. So are Edgar's "borne," the amount that Lear has "seen," the life he has most vibrantly, enduringly "lived." The further wonder is that we, like them, have witnessed and survived this wonder.

Five

The Image of
the Family in
King Lear

Thomas McFarland

King Lear develops its action along a pattern supplied simultaneously by poetic fantasy and by historical reality. In the main plot, the relationship between Lear and his daughters is prefigured in the record of a distressed family situation of the late Elizabethan period. Brian Annesley, who for many years had been a gentleman pensioner to Queen Elizabeth, had three daughters. As he grew old, Annesley's mind began to give way, and two of his daughters, Christian, who was the wife of Lord Sandys of the Essex Rebellion, and Lady Grace Wildgoose, petitioned to have the old man declared insane and his estate placed in the care of Lady Wildgoose's husband. Annesley's third daughter, who was named Cordell or Cordelia, opposed the action and in October 1603 sent a letter to Cecil on behalf of her "poor aged and daily dying father." History does not inform us of the ending of this family turbulence, other than that, when Annesley died in 1604, Lady Wildgoose unsuccessfully challenged his will. Some scholars think that when the Fool comments on the alliance of Regan and Goneril in the second act of the play, he is obliquely alluding to the Annesley affair in the line "Winter's not gone yet, if the wild geese fly that way" (2.4.45).

To this prototype for the main plot of *King Lear* drawn from the quotidian reality of family life in Shakespeare's milieu we may add a fictional prototype for the subplot, drawn from the furthest reaches of Elizabethan familial fantasy. For the story of Gloucester and his two sons is taken from what Sidney called "this idle worke of mine," "this child, which I am loath to father," this "trifle, and that triflinglie handled," that is, *The Arcadia*. Here, in 1590, in the tenth chapter of the second book, we read of

> an aged man, and a young, scarcely come to the age of a man, both poorely arayed, extreamely weather-beaten; the olde man blinde, the young man leading him: and yet through all those miseries, in both these seemed to appeare a kind of noblenesse, not sutable to that affliction. But the first words they heard, were these of the old man. . . . feare not, my miserie cannot be greater than it is, & nothing doth become me but miserie; feare not the danger of my blind steps, I cannot fall worse than I am. And doo not I pray thee, do not obstinately continue to infect thee with my wretchedness.

The young man then tells the observers how this doleful scene came about:

> This old man (whom I leade) was lately rightfull Prince of this countrie of *Paphlagonia*, by the hard-harted ungratefulnes of a sonne of his, deprived, not onely of his kingdome (whereof no forraine forces were ever able to spoyle him) but of his sight, the riches which Nature graûts to the poorest creatures. Whereby, & by other his unnaturall dealings, he hath bin driven to such griefe, as even now he would have had me to have led him to the toppe of this rocke, thêce to cast himselfe headlong to death: and so would have made me (who received my life of him) to be the worker of his destruction.

The "toppe of this rocke" in this passage becomes, in Shakespeare's imaginative expansion, the powerful evocation by which Edgar deludes his blinded father (and more than one modern critic) into thinking he stands on the cliffs of Dover:

Come on, sir; here's the place: stand still. How fearful
And dizzy 'tis to cast one's eyes so low!
. . . .
                              Half way down
Hangs one that gathers sampire, dreadful trade!
Methinks he seems no bigger than his head.
The fishermen that walk upon the beach
Appear like mice; and yond tall anchoring bark
Diminished to her cock; her cock, a buoy
Almost too small for sight. The murmuring surge
That on th' unnumb'red idle pebble chafes
Cannot be heard so high.

(4.6.11-22)

Shakespeare's conception of what Edgar immediately after-ward calls "the extreme verge" is thus directly linked to Sidney's fantasy, as we can see again in the play's expansion of the blind king's lament as formulated by Sidney: "my miserie cannot be greater than it is, & nothing doth become me but miserie. . . . I cannot fall worse than I am." For Edgar in effect supplies a commentary: "Who is't can say, 'I am at the worst'? / I am worse than e'er I was. . . . And worse I may be yet: the worst is not / So long as we can say, 'This is the worst' " (4.1.25-28).

King Lear, to take up Edgar's rhetoric of descent, is both a drama of "the extreme verge" and an extended trope of things getting worse. We might indeed say of its depiction of life that "This is the worst," except that to say so would be to turn us to Edgar's wisdom and make us realize that *Hamlet* may descend beyond even that description. Certainly over both plays there broods Hamlet's disbelieving realization "That it should come to this." In this statement, the sense of moving from hope to horror is accentuated by the stunning virtuosity of Shakespeare's rendering of happy past and ter-rible present by the pain-blurred pronouns of "it" and "this."

Both plays augment their pain by fostering it in the matrix of family life. After this initial congruence, however, the fa-milial similarities diminish. The family situation in *Hamlet*

follows the model of Senecan tragedy, which in its turn had
its eye upon Greek tragedy, especially the familial horrors of
the house of Atreus. Seneca, who is a much more considerable
dramatist than is at present fashionable to believe (Scaliger,
who did not take these things lightly, ranked him with Eu-
ripides), considered human life to be hell on earth.[1] In this
line of genesis, the family situation in *Hamlet*, to adopt a
modern perspective, can be not inappropriately summed up
in the vision of R. D. Laing: "A family can act as gangsters,
offering each other mutual protection against each other's
violence. It is a reciprocal terrorism." Or again:

> From the moment of birth, when the Stone Age baby
> confronts the twentieth-century mother, the baby is sub-
> jected to those forces of violence, called love, as its mother
> and father . . . have been. These forces are mainly con-
> cerned with destroying most of its potentialities, and on
> the whole this enterprise is successful. By the time the
> new human being is fifteen or so, we are left with a being
> like ourselves, a half-crazed creature more or less adjusted
> to a mad world.[2]

The latter part of Laing's formula for modern youth, "a half-

---

[1] Commentators have said little on this matter, although the cumulative
testimony of the plays is almost overwhelming. But compare a philosophical
analyst's recent observation with respect to Seneca's statement that it is wrong
to hate life too much: "The remark gives him away; his own view is based
on a hatred of life. . . . Fundamentally Seneca's wise man is in love with
death. He is looking out for a tolerable pretext to die." J. M. Rist, *Stoic
Philosophy* (Cambridge: Cambridge Univ. Press, 1969), p. 249. For Scaliger's
judgment of Seneca, see J. W. Cunliffe, *The Influence of Seneca on Elizabethan
Tragedy* (1893; reprint ed., Hamden, Conn.: Archon Books, 1965), p. 7.

[2] *The Politics of Experience* (New York: Pantheon, 1967), pp. 59, 36. The
reciprocal terrorism can be physical as well as mental, and it is certainly not
limited to twentieth-century realities. Thus, for a single emphatic instance,
Augustin Thierry records in his *Récits des temps mérovingiens* that, "in the
year 561, after an expedition against one of his sons, whose rebellion he
punished by having him burned at the stake together with his wife and
children, Lothar, perfectly at ease in mind and conscience, returned to his
house at Braine." (I have used the translation by M.F.O. Jenkins.)

crazed creature more or less adjusted to a mad world," might serve as a rough description of the situation of Hamlet himself.

The model of the family in *King Lear* is different. The play itself might be seen as an exalted version of the "domestic tragedy" of the period—as an elevated form of such structures as *A Woman Killed with Kindness* or even *Arden of Feversham*. The situation in *Hamlet*, by contrast, is almost flamboyant; it has the specialness of things that happen only once, in the realm of the hypothetical, and to others than ourselves. It is significant that the play has been approached through such pairings as "Hamlet and Orestes" and "Hamlet and Oedipus." When Freud first discerned the outline of the Oedipus complex, which he was forced to see as a flaw at the very root of human nature, he immediately illustrated it by reference to Hamlet. And the form of our contemplation of such shattering familial pain as that represented by Orestes and Oedipus is the aesthetic distancing described by Kant, whereby we take pleasure in catastrophic events such as hurricanes and erupting volcanoes provided we are simultaneously secure from their consequences. A shipwreck happens to others, not to us; and Oedipus, Orestes, and Hamlet find themselves in unthinkable situations that accentuate our own security as spectators. In this same context, we may note that of all Freud's insights into human nature, none has more fiercely engaged our protective mechanisms of resistance and denial than has his formulation of the Oedipus complex. It was not merely Malinowski who professed to find no such complex in the primitive societies he studied; almost every soi-disant rectifier of Freud begins by denying the universality of the Oedipus complex. It is as though we think it suitable for Oedipus, but not for us. We are not Prince Hamlet, nor were we meant to be.

The situation in *King Lear* involves a different model of experience, an image of family life that is neither flamboyant nor unique. On the contrary, it is in significant respects almost commonplace. Lear's pain and outrage are larger versions of the pain and outrage that almost all parents at some point and to some degree experience because of their offspring.

Lear's agonized realization that "Age is unnecessary" is encountered again and again by aging parents and grandparents
faced with loss of prestige and function, and possibly with
transportation to homes for the elderly. Goneril's impatience
with Lear's residing in her own domicile is an immensely
larger version of a commonplace experience, that of the strains
resulting when an aged parent takes up residence with a married child. "Let me not stay a jot for dinner; go, get it ready"
(1.4.8-9), orders Lear imperiously, after the audience has just
been informed of Goneril's instructions to "prepare for dinner" (1.3.27). This embryonic family clash, the experience of
untold numbers of housewives and aging parents writ large,
is the antipode of the poison coursing like quicksilver through
the porches of ears that we find in Hamlet's context. "By day
and night he wrongs me," flashes Goneril, her very accents
being those of the harried and hateful, but by the same token
those of the commonplace and oft-repeated:

> I'll not endure it.
> His knights grow riotous, and himself upbraids us
> On every trifle. When he returns from hunting,
> I will not speak with him. Say I am sick.
> If you come slack of former services,
> You shall do well; the fault of it I'll answer.
>
> (1.3.6-11)

The same tone of quotidian exasperation permeates Goneril's spiteful references to her father's Fool:

> Not only, sir, this your all-licensed Fool,
> But other of your insolent retinue
> Do hourly carp and quarrel, breaking forth
> In rank and not-to-be-endurèd riots.
>
> (1.4.201-204)

Unlovable though she is, Goneril here speaks in tones with
which many with numerous and long-staying guests can sym-
pathize, and we do remember that previously she has taken
care to ascertain at least one of the facts: "Did my father
strike my gentleman for chiding of his Fool?" "Ay, madam,"

comes the answer (1.3.1-3). Moreover, in the early part of the play's action she speaks in tones that at least attempt to justify her conduct:

> I do beseech you
> To understand my purposes aright.
> As you are old and reverend, should be wise.
> Here do you keep a hundred knights and squires,
> Men so disordered, so deboshed, and bold,
> That this our court, infected with their manners,
> Shows like a riotous inn. Epicurism and lust
> Makes it more like a tavern or a brothel
> Than a graced palace.
>
> (1.4.239-247)

Lear reacts like many a parent, and entirely like his own self-indulgent early self; we do not here have his later "O, I have ta'en / Too little care of this," but rather instant righteousness and thunderbolts:

> Darkness and devils!
> Saddle my horses; call my train together.
> Degenerate bastard, I'll not trouble thee:
> Yet have I left a daughter.
>
> (1.4.253-256)

In this instance, Lear's manipulation of the dynamics of family favoritism, which repeats the fatuity with which he had offered Cordelia "a third more opulent than your sisters" (1.1.86), elicits from Goneril the shrill and wonderful rejoinder—wonderful because it endures in the common situations of human experience:

> You strike my people, and your disordered rabble
> Make servants of their betters.
>
> (1.4.257-258)

It is because of the repeated projection of such exquisitely nuanced appeals to the *sensus communis* (Kant says that "by the name *sensus communis* is to be understood the idea of a *public* sense, i.e. a critical faculty which in its reflective act

97

takes account [*a priori*] of the mode of representation of every one else, in order, *as it were*, to weigh its judgment with the collective reason of mankind") that the situation between Lear and his daughters cannot rewardingly be described in terms of the rhetoric of good and evil. Thus Maynard Mack's reference, in his *King Lear in Our Time*, to "the unmitigated badness of Goneril and Regan" seems somewhat beside the point. Moreover, his belief that the two sisters represent "paradigms of evil" leads in my opinion to a subtle misconception of the play's meaning. In the rudimentary morality dramas that in some sense form an adumbrative basis of *King Lear*, such figures would indeed be paradigms of evil; in the two-dimensional fairy-tale motif of Lear's processional entrance at the beginning and his arbitrary dividing of his kingdom into three (an action of the same order as Old King Cole summoning his fiddlers three), Goneril and Regan do assume the roles of wicked elder sisters to the Cinderella-like good third sister. But these are lower layers and starting points, not the profound process of the play itself. In that process, as I have elsewhere urged, good and evil are conceptions with little purchase.[3]

If we persist in using the conventional rhetoric of good and evil, we should, of course, certainly have to stigmatize Goneril, Regan, and Edmund as evil. But by that same schematism we should also be forced to think of Lear and Gloucester as good. How unfitting this latter conception would be can perhaps be indicated in brief by returning to the source of the subplot. In *The Arcadia* the son who is helping his blind father says: "noble Gentlemen . . . if either of you have a father, and feele what deutifull affection is engraffed in a sonnes hart, let me intreate you to convey this afflicted Prince to some place of rest & securitie." What Sidney next writes should prompt our reflection on its probable function in Shakespeare's work: "But before they could make him answere his father began to speake, Ah my sonne (said he) how evill an Historian are

---

[3] "Reduction and Renewal in *King Lear*," in *Tragic Meanings in Shakespeare* (New York: Random House, 1966).

you, that leave out the chief knotte of all the discourse? *my* wickednes, *my* wickednes."

In the movement of the play, as opposed to the source, the wickedness of the father is finally no more relevant than the evil of the child. What we are presented instead is an image of the family in dynamic interaction, an image intensified and underscored by being doubled into parallel plots. The process of things getting worse is coordinate with a process of progressive deterioration and dereliction in family relationships. After all, the source of the play found in Geoffrey of Monmouth specifically includes the allegedly evil Goneril and Regan in the original unity of love: "He was without Male Issue," says that source for *King Lear*, "but had three Daughters whose Names were Gonorilla, Regan, and Cordeilla, of whom he was doatingly fond, but especially of his youngest Cordeilla." It is hardly an exaggeration, indeed, to say that the subject of the play is, not the agony of the king, but the agony of the family; and in a very real sense the protagonist of the play is not Lear alone, nor even Lear and Gloucester in tandem, but the two fathers as the center of family relationships and the service relationships that pertain to them. Any impact on any strand of this web of relationships perturbs the whole; when Gloucester suffers, a nameless serving man lays down his life in sympathetic response.

The protagonistic function is thus dispersed, and the dispersal is both welcome and in a sense necessary because of the unattractiveness of age. Although the fact that Lear is a man standing on the outer edge of existence—"O, sir, you are old," notes Regan, "Nature in you stands on the very verge / Of his confine" (2.4.143-145)—gives him immense tragic authenticity and the play immense leverage at the tragic intersection of being and nonbeing, by the same token, his standing at the verge of nature's confine makes it difficult for us to identify with him. For an aged man is but a paltry thing, and Lear's prospects on his very verge are as bleak as those of Gloucester on his own extreme verge. The motifs of "very verge" and "extreme verge," though emphasized by the aged fathers, actually pertain to all the characters and in truth to all human existence: in this life we all stand on the razor's edge, and death has a thousand doors. But it is Lear's definition as father that connects him with younger life and its attendant hope. His fatherhood draws him back into our common ken; his familial identity ropes him to the others as he teeters on the edge of the abyss.[4] Indeed, even Regan's heartless remark quoted above would not have been made were he not her father.

The tension between Lear's two roles in life, one as king with its patina of symbolic paternalism, the other as father to a specific family, generates the tragic situation that arises in the play. Or more exactly, it makes up the tragic abscissa that, along with the tragic ordinate constituted by being's straining against nonbeing, delimits *King Lear's* tragic space.

Lear pervasively assumes at the outset that his status as king and his status as father are the same, and this initial confusion leads him into the fallacious assumption that power and love are interchangeable.[5] It is not merely that he mis-

[4] Compare, for example, William R. Elton: "Paralleled by Edgar's quest for identity, Lear demands his own identity of daughters, his retainers, his Fool, and himself. . . . From one point of view, indeed, Lear may be said sequentially to dissociate into his children, Goneril and Regan (selfish willfulness) and Cordelia (courageous adamancy), as Gloucester may be seen successively to dissolve into his components, Edmund (lust) and Edgar (pathos). Here, fatherhood, as in Dostoievsky's Karamazov family, involves not only the problem of identity but also that of identity in multiplicity. Thus, through self-alienation and division, characters generate proxies for themselves, as well as analogues of each other." *"King Lear" and the Gods* (San Marino, Calif.: Huntington Library, 1968), p. 280.

[5] Underlying the whole structure of Elizabethan attitudes about the nature of kingship was the implicit *analogia* of king with father (and of both with God). Thus, for instance, James VI composes his *Basilikon Doron* in the dual role of father counseling son and of king instructing subject (as we can see from the subtitle of the 1603 edition: *His Maiesties Instrvctions to his Dearest Sonne, Henry the Prince*). Furthermore, though the analogy of king and father was so taken for granted that explicit statements are infrequent, oblique alignments abound, e.g. "A good King (thinking his highest honour to consist in the due discharge of his calling) employeth all his studie and paines, to procure and mainteine (by the making and execution of good lawes) the welfare and peace of his people, and (as their naturall father and kindly maister) thinketh his greatest contentment standeth in their prosperitie, and his greatest suretie in hauing their hearts." Or again: "Ye see nowe (my Sonne) how (for

takenly believes that so much love can equal so much land, or that he carries the confusion between love and power into the further quantification of the hundred knights, appurtenances necessary to a king but irrelevant to a father. Rather, it is that he believes that the attributes he gives up as king are ones he can retain solely as father: "I do invest you jointly with my power, / Preeminence, and all the large effects / That troop with majesty," he says to Goneril and Regan and their husbands:

> Ourself, by monthly course,
> With reservation of an hundred knights,
> By you to be sustained, shall our abode
> Make with you by due turn. Only we shall retain
> The name, and all th' addition to a king.
> (1.1.130-136)

---

the zeale I beare to acquent you with the plain & single verity of al things) I haue not spared to playe the baird against all the estates of my kingdome: but I protest before God, I do it with the fatherly loue that I owe to them all, onely hating their vices, whereof there is a good number of honest men freed in euery estate." *Basilikon Doron*, reprint of 1599 edition, pp. 29 (sig. E3), 64 (sig. 14). But however much, under the most benign interpretation of their possibilities, the roles of king and father may be thought to coincide, in actual fact the absolute power of a king ill accords with the loving flexibility of a father. The dynamics of the contrast are existential, not historical or time-bound by Elizabethan convention. Thus a prominent modern psychiatrist prefaces a well-known study of the genesis of schizophrenia within a family by a description of the father that timelessly describes Lear's own preoccupation with his appurtenances as a king: "The father . . . thought of himself as a great man and expected his family to support his narcissistic need for admiration. He was unable to recognize the needs of others or even realize that they viewed the world differently than he did." Theodore Lidz, Preface to *A Mingled Yarn: Chronicle of a Troubled Family*, by Beulah Parker (New Haven: Yale Univ. Press, 1972), p. xi. In this context, it is interesting to remind ourselves that James, unlike the Lear of the play's opening, insists that a king should be humble, because a king is simply an ordinary man called to eminence by God: "Foster true Humilitie in banishing pride," and "when ye ar there, remember the throne is Gods and not yours, that ye sit in." *Basilikon Doron*, pp. 115 (sig. Q2), 109-110 (sig. P3). In brief, whatever the identity of kingship and fatherhood in static conception, the formula that describes their functioning interaction is this: the more king, the less father; the more father, the less king.

As Lawrence Stone observes, from a vantage ground atop a mass of sociohistorical data: "Shakespeare's interpretation of King Lear merely underscores the moral that a father who gives up real power, in the expectation of obtaining the love and attention of his children instead, is merely exhibiting a form of insanity. His inevitable disappointment would have come as no surprise to an Elizabethan audience."[6] Nor to a modern one either, we might append.

We see the same confusion of Lear's conception of himself as king and as father in his decision to divide his kingdom into three, a decision that violated the accumulated wisdom of Elizabethan statecraft. As Sir Thomas Elyot said in 1531, in *The Boke Named the Gouernour*:

> Lyke as to a castell or fortresse suffisethe one owner or soueraygne and where any mo be of like power and authoritie seldome cometh the warke to perfection. . . . In semblable wyse doth a publike weale that hath mo chiefe gouernours than one.

He goes on to say that "if any desireth to haue the gouernance of one persone proued by histories let him fyrste resorte to the holy scripture; where he shall fynde that almyghty god commanded Moses . . . gyuynge onely to hym that authoritie without appoyntynge to hym any other assistence of equall power or dignitie." After many examples of the ills attendant upon divided rule, he says,

> But what nede we to serche so ferre from vs sens we haue sufficient examples nere vnto us? . . . After that the Saxons by treason had expelled out of Englande the Britons whiche were the auncient inhabitantes: this realme was deuyded in to sondry regions or kyngdomes. O what mysery was the people then in: O howe this most noble Isle of the worlde was decerpt and rent in pieces.

Elyot's political admonitions find confirmation in 1561 in

[6] *The Family, Sex and Marriage in England, 1500-1800* (New York: Harper and Row, 1977), p. 97.

Sackville's and Norton's *Gorboduc,* where the choric counselor warns:

> To part your realm unto my lords, your sons,
> I think not good for you, ne yet for them,
> But worst of all for this our native land.
> Within one land one single rule is best.
> Divided reigns do make divided hearts,
> But peace preserves the country and the prince.
> (1.2.256-261)

In 1599, finally, to trace the unanimity of opinion into Shakespeare's own day, King James VI wrote to his son in the
Basilikon Doron:

> Make your eldest sonne ISAAC, leauing him all your
> Kingdomes, and prouide the rest with priuate posses-
> siones: otherwayes by deuiding your Kingdomes, yee
> shall leaue the seede of diuisione and discorde among
> your posteritie.

Lear, in short, is behaving like a father and not like a king
when he divides his kingdom. The inadequacy of his action
purely as that of a father, as opposed to its patent folly as the
decision of a king, is attendant, not upon the division as such,
but rather upon the inequality of the division, that is, the
doting promise to Cordelia to give her "a third more opulent
than your sisters," a third that directly validates Goneril's
once resentful but by now matter-of-fact realization that "he
always loved our sister most" (1.1.290).

An even more damaging result of Lear's confusion of kingship and fatherhood is his feeling that, like a monarch, but
not like a father, he can abrogate the ties of kinship. But the
family has its deep-rooted sanctities. The original sin of this
dark cosmos is constituted by Lear's denial of family relation
in his rejection of Cordelia:

> Here I disclaim all my paternal care,
> Propinquity and property of blood,
> And as a stranger to my heart and me

Hold thee from this for ever.
                    (1.1.113-116)

Thus Lear's action, not in becoming angry with Cordelia, who has herself acted with some of the old man's willfulness, but in disclaiming paternal care, propinquity, and property of blood, is, if we like the rhetoric of good and evil, the beginning of the evil in the play's progression of events; it is an action of the same order as those of Goneril and Regan. Lear's own violation is eventually redeemed, and its purgation begins with his dawning realization that "I did her wrong" (1.5.24); whereas Goneril and Regan cannot escape their own selves and eventually begin to prey upon each other, in Albany's phrase, "like monsters of the deep." Albany's terrifying image, which is the nadir of the play's animal references and alludes to the unspoken, dreaded boundary situation of possible descent from true human relation, is prefigured by Lear's violation at the beginning of the play. Thus France observes that Cordelia, as "the best, the dearest," could not "commit a thing so monstrous" (1.1.217) as Lear's reaction suggests; and he refers to her "offense" as being of "unnatural degree / That monsters it" (1.1.218-220) if Lear is to be thought justified. The same misconception and foreshadowing attend also on Gloucester's early self-indulgence: "He cannot be such a monster," he exclaims of Edgar; "Nor is not, sure," replies Edmund smoothly (1.2.97-98). Still again, the image is refocused when Lear speaks of Goneril's ingratitude as more hideous "in a child / Than the sea-monster!" (1.4.262-263).

Thus Lear's initial confusion as to what pertains to a king and what pertains to a father sets in motion the tragic descent. That he does confuse these roles points us to a truth about the structure of the family as presented in this play. That structure, as we have suggested, is fundamentally different from the Senecan flamboyance of the family in *Hamlet*. The tradition there is one in which Titus Andronicus can at the very outset of his play execute Tamora's son Alarbus ("Alarbus' limbs are lopped," report his sons matter-of-factly), despite her piteous pleas to spare him. Shortly thereafter Titus imperiously slays his own son Mutius. The play, adding the horrors of Ovid to those of Seneca, proceeds from this bloody beginning into a bizarre sequence of massacres along family lines. To reinvoke the phrase of R. D. Laing, this conception of the family exhibits on its face the contours of "reciprocal terrorism"; and it is this conception, though immensely refined, that obtains in *Hamlet*.

The family image in *King Lear* is much more like a different kind of ancient paradigm: that serene structure of mutual regard revealed in Plutarch's letter to his wife on the death of one of their children. Or to summon a modern reference to counterbalance Laing, the family image in *King Lear* is what in Christopher Lasch's rubric is termed "haven in a heartless world." It is to seek a haven that Lear gives up his crown:

> Know that we have divided
> In three our kingdom; and 'tis our fast intent
> To shake all cares and business from our age,
> Conferring them on younger strengths.
>
> (1.1.37-40)

"I loved her most," he says of Cordelia, "and thought to set my rest / On her kind nursery" (1.1.123-124).

That the family here is conceived of as a haven in a heartless world is not contradicted by the fact that the horrors later perpetrated within that family vie with and in certain senses even surpass those in *Hamlet*. For what we are talking about is, not the reality of family life, but merely the proffered image of the family. In truth, the conception of family as a haven in a heartless world can in certain respects lead to greater even though less visible destructions than can less affecting images, even as an explosion of dynamite is augmented if the explosive is covered. The offices of psychoanalysts are thronged with tormented patients who bear witness to this truth, and its dimensions are cogently revealed by the nineteenth-century diarist Amiel:

Oh, the family! If the pious, traditional superstition with

which we envelop this institution would let us tell the truth about the matter, what a reckoning it would have to settle! What numberless martyrdoms it has required, dissemblingly, inexorably! How many hearts have been stifled by it, lacerated and broken. . . . The family may be all that is best in this world, but too often it is all that is worst. . . . The truth is that the family relation exists only to put us to the proof and that it gives us infinitely more suffering than happiness.

In this context we see Goneril, Regan, and Edmund all as victims of the family situation. Their inadequate action is somewhat like that of Joseph's brothers, rendered envious and malicious by their father's favoritism, or even like that of another family victim named Cain.

Despite their differences in image and provenance, the family structures in *King Lear* and in *Hamlet* both generate tragic intensifications. In one way, moreover, the two structures are identical. For both are broken families at the outset, and broken in complementary ways. In *Hamlet* there is no father, in *King Lear* no mother. We think of correlates everywhere in Shakespeare, so quickly, indeed, that we are overwhelmed by the intuition that a very substantial portion of Shakespeare's literary energy was discharged through varying apprehensions of the dynamics of family structures. Almost all these families are also broken. We think of Bertram and his mother the Countess Rousillon, with their situation, as well as that of Helena, depending on a dead father. We think of Coriolanus and his mother, Volumnia, again with a dead father. We think yet again of Brabantio and Desdemona, with a dead mother, of Polonius and Ophelia, again with a dead mother, and, perhaps most compellingly of all and most germane to the situation in *King Lear*, of Prospero and Miranda, still again with a dead mother.

These relationships are for Shakespeare typically charged with the most electric emotions. It is perhaps not entirely accidental that his series of passionate sonnets to a young friend involves a recognition of the emotional bond between

the youth and his mother, with apparently no father to consider: "Is it for fear to wet a widow's eye," he asks in the
ninth sonnet, "That thou consum'st thyself in single life? /
Ah, if thou issueless shalt hap to die, / The world will wail thee
like a makeless wife; / The world will be thy widow and still
weep." But possibly the most unmistakable index of the cen-
trality of family kinesis in Shakespeare's concern is the scene
in the fourth act of *King Lear* where Lear is reunited with
Cordelia. Such a theme of reunion, and especially of the reunion of a family—or, as here, the living heart of a family—
mines the deepest and richest lode of Shakespeare's affirmation of life; and that truth is apparent in other places than
King Lear. In the vast tropes of reunion and reconciliation
that conclude the action of Shakespeare's last comedies, the
most intense themes of joy appear, and they are invariably
generated by the resurgence of a family relationship.[7] Thus
Leontes, having seemingly destroyed both his wife and his
daughter, finds his daughter again in the lost Perdita and his
wife again in the statue suddenly come to life. The language
of joy in the familial reconstitution is almost overpowering;
it is presented as a climax beyond even the reunion of friends
as celebrated by the meeting of Leontes and Polixenes:

> Did you see the meeting of the two kings? . . . Then have
> you lost a sight which was to be seen, cannot be spoken
> of. There might you have beheld one joy crown another
> . . . their joy waded in tears. . . . Our king, being ready
> to leap out of himself for joy of his found daughter . . .
> then asks Bohemia forgiveness.
>
> (*The Winter's Tale*, 5.2.41-54)

As the almost orgiastic description continues, the final points
of reference are familial. For the clown says:

[7] Though Stanley Wells has pointed out that the joyous reconciliation scenes
in the last comedies are prefigured by such scenes in the Greek romances that
lie behind them, we may take it as an axiom of Shakespearean interpretation
that what Shakespeare chooses to retain from his source materials is as truly
representative of his intent as are themes created by his imagination ex nihilo.

The king's son took me by the hand and called me
brother; and then the two kings called my father brother;
and then the prince, (my brother) and the princess (my
sister) called my father father.

(*The Winter's Tale*, 5.2.143-147)

This joy is confirmed and if possible even surpassed in the
familial reconstitution of *Pericles*. First Pericles is reunited
with his daughter Marina:

O Helicanus, strike me, honored sir!
Give me a gash, put me to present pain;
Lest this great sea of joys rushing upon me
O'erbear the shores of my mortality,
And drown me with their sweetness. O, come hither,
Thou that beget'st him that did thee beget;
Thou that wast born at sea, buried at Tharsus,
And found at sea again!

(5.1.194-201)

I embrace you.
Give me my robes. I am wild in my beholding.
O heavens bless my girl!

(5.1.225-227)

The reunion with the daughter Marina is followed by reunion
with the wife Thaisa:

This, this! No more. You gods, your present kindness
Makes my past miseries sports. You shall do well
That on the touching of her lips I may
Melt and no more be seen.

(5.3.39-42)

And yet not even in these outpourings of joy and wonder
is the emotion as powerful as in the awesome reconciliation
scene between Lear and Cordelia. Lear's awakening from
madness into rationality is, on the literal plane, a moment of
restoration, reconciliation, and reunion. But on the anagogical
plane it is more; it is the reawakening of the dead into paradise.
Lear's confused words on regaining consciousness reverberate
with the sweetest *topoi* of Christian hope:

You do me wrong to take me out o' th' grave.
Thou art a soul in bliss.

(4.7.45-46)

When Cordelia asks, "Sir, do you know me?" Lear's answer is "You are a spirit, I know. Where did you die?" (4.7.48-49). Shakespeare's astonishing evocation of the varieties of human tears in the remainder of the passage achieves a finality that suggests the supervening state of paradise, which, in the words of the Book of Revelation hauntingly taken up by Milton, will wipe the tears forever from our eyes. Lear first speaks of tears:

> I am bound
> Upon a wheel of fire, that mine own tears
> Do scald like molten lead.

(4.7.46-48)

The connection between scalding past and paradisal renewal is sealed by tears of watering restoration, as revealed by the virtuosity (never enough admired) of Cordelia's tear-choked replies "And so I am, I am," and "No cause, no cause":

LEAR.   Do not laugh at me,
For, as I am a man, I think this lady
To be my child Cordelia.
CORDELIA.   And so I am, I am.
LEAR. Be your tears wet? Yes, faith. I pray, weep not.
If you have poison for me, I will drink it.
I know you do not love me; for your sisters
Have, as I do remember, done me wrong.
You have some cause, they have not.
CORDELIA.   No cause, no cause.

(4.7.68-75)

Art can hardly go beyond this. Both the literal and the anagogic planes are superintended by the Doctor, who naturally would stand by a sick man recovering consciousness (even though this doctor's sudden prominence is mysterious). But as I have elsewhere pointed out, this sudden figure takes up the function of the doctor from the English folk play or

109

mummer's play, who, as E. K. Chambers records, abruptly appears to restore the slain duelist to life.

But doctors also assist at childbirth, and that additional function leads us to still another level of meaning in this supreme scene of reconciliation. For Lear is not merely the sick and confused man regaining consciousness and rationality. He is here not restricted even to the deeper motif of devastated mortal reborn to heaven's bliss. He is also, in palpable respects, the child entering the world for the first time; and Cordelia, hovering over his bed, is, in awesome psycho-dramatic recapitulation, the eternal mother brooding over the infant's crib. Earlier in the play age was equated with infancy in the statement "Old fools are babes again" (1.3.20), and just before the reconciliation scene there is insistent reference to our entrance into the world:

> We came crying hither:
> Thou know'st, the first time that we smell the air
> We wawl and cry. . . .
> . . . .
> When we are born, we cry that we are come
> To this great stage of fools.
>
> (4.6.178-183)

These images subliminally join with the tears of the restoration scene, for Lear's tears that scald like molten lead, though unforgettably part of the agony and guilt through which he has passed, are no more scalding than the infant's tears at birth. And the very indications by which we see Lear purged of his madness and spleen are also coordinate with the sense of infant joy and calm. The doctor informs us that "the great rage . . . is killed in him" (4.7.78-79). A "very foolish fond old man" who reiterates that "I am old and foolish," who asks others to "bear with me," to "forget and forgive" (4.7.60, 83-84), is a man who in essential respects resumes the relationships of his earliest life.

I have dwelt on this one supreme scene to make clear the enormous charge of emotion with which it is invested. Its recapitulation of the earliest family situation of mother and child, which receives additional emphasis from the absence of Cordelia's mother and Lear's wife throughout the play, leads us to understand how the scene can plumb such psychic depth. At the same time, we realize that the recreation of the child's union with the parent is precisely, in Freud's description, the impelling origin and ultimate goal in the sexual development of every human being.

This aperture of understanding provided by the third or recapitulative plane of the reconciliation scene reveals to us another aspect of the play's meaning as well. For it occurs to every careful critic that there is at least a surface anomaly in the play: *King Lear*, which is arguably the greatest of all human documents, largely dispenses with the sexual relationships of mankind. There is no proper vehicle here for love between the sexes. It is not simply that the nominal protagonist, Lear, is eighty years old; it is also that such interest seems deliberately to be evicted. The king of France, for instance, speaks in the idealistic language of Sonnet 116, paralleling its insistence that "love is not love / Which alters when it alteration finds" with "Love's not love / When it is mingled with regards that stands / Aloof from th' entire point" (1.1.238-240). But after thus displaying his own true understanding of love, the king of France withdraws to his own country, taking love with him. The possibilities for love thenceforth largely devolve on Edmund, and they become, not an index of idealistic intensification, but a grotesque badge of deterioration: "To both these sisters have I sworn my love; / Each jealous of the other, as the stung / Are of the adder" (5.1.56-58). This seething sexuality is further removed from the nobly human by Lear's searing hallucination:

> I pardon that man's life. What was thy cause?
> Adultery?
> Thou shalt not die: die for adultery! No:
> The wren goes to't, and the small gilded fly
> Does lecher in my sight.
> Let copulation thrive; for Gloucester's bastard son
> Was kinder to his father than my daughters

Got 'tween the lawful sheets.
To't, luxury, pell-mell! for I lack soldiers.
Behold yond simp'ring dame,
Whose face between her forks presages snow,
That minces virtue, and does shake the head
To hear of pleasure's name.
The fitchew, nor the soilèd horse, goes to't
With a more riotous appetite.
Down from the waist they are Centaurs,
Though women all above:
But to the girdle do the gods inherit,
Beneath is all the fiend's.
There's hell, there's darkness, there is the sulphurous pit,
burning, scalding, stench, consumption; fie, fie, fie! pah,
pah! Give me an ounce of civet; good apothecary, sweeten
my imagination.

(4.6.109-131)

And when Gloucester then comments, "O let me kiss that
hand!" Lear's reply reverberates with sublime disgust: "Let
me wipe it first; it smells of mortality."

The disgust with which the horizontal and procreative ac-
tivities of man are here viewed tends to strengthen the urgency
of the vertical and familial affections. The same disgust is
expressed by Shakespeare in other places: in his Sonnet 129,
for instance, or in the poisoned imaginations of Leontes and
Othello; most of all, perhaps, in Hamlet's interview with his
mother:

Nay, but to live
In the rank sweat of an enseamèd bed,
Stewed in corruption, honeying and making love
Over the nasty sty.

(3.4.92-95)

And when Gertrude asks, "What shall I do?" Hamlet answers
that she should not

Let the bloat king tempt you again to bed,
Pinch wanton on your cheek, call you his mouse,

And let him, for a pair of reechy kisses,
Or paddling in your neck with his damned fingers,
Make you to ravel all this matter out,
That I essentially am not in madness,
But mad in craft.

(3.4.183-189)

This vividly expressed sexual disgust functions in similar ways in both *Hamlet* and *King Lear*; it tends to displace Gertrude as paramour of Claudius and reinstate and emphasize Gertrude as wife of the father, as matron of the family, as mother of the son. The sexual disgust of *King Lear*, in the same way, should be seen as not merely a profound expression of something in the man Shakespeare himself, although I have no doubt that it is that as well, but also as a deliberate eviction from the play of the only force that in both common experience and psychological observation challenges the satisfactions and securities of the family. For whatever Shakespeare's idiosyncratic disgust with human sexuality (as we see, for instance, in Sonnet 94), he was also capable of depicting sexuality in the most radiant terms, as *Romeo and Juliet* and *Antony and Cleopatra* attest. We are reminded, nevertheless, that in both these plays the apotheosis of sexuality occurs explicitly at the expense of family solidarity. Yet by the same token, the fact that sexual disgust appears with jolting power in *King Lear* tends to reassert the primary importance of the ties of the family relationship.

If in *King Lear* the sexual interest largely devolves on Edmund and thereby becomes an insignia of deterioration, Edmund's position as bastard both threatens the normative structure of the family and reveals him as the initial legatee of family pain. He thereby becomes the leader, as it were, the first in line, of those who descend toward the disintegrative bleakness of the world of storm and night. But in his descent he is unable to purge himself and forge a new being. Hence Edmund also, like Goneril and Regan, is less rewardingly viewed as evil than as inadequate. Indeed, he is a figure invested with deep pathos.

113

Here again an examination of the two sources to which I referred at the beginning of this lecture is revealing. For the Annesley prototype differs from the other sources in that it alone presents the old man as infirm of mind (his daughter Cordell writes Cecil that her father's "many years service to our late dread Sovereign Mistress" deserved better than "at his last gasp to be recorded and registered a Lunatic"); it thereby enlists our universal or public sympathy with the plight of the old man and our outrage at the callousness of Lady Wildgoose. In the source for the subplot, however, something is absent rather than present; there is no bastard, and this fact paradoxically makes the figure of Edmund seem somehow more important in Shakespeare's design.

If, as I have been tacitly assuming and sometimes hinting, Shakespeare's almost obsessive preoccupation with dramatic structures of the family takes its enormous emotional force from his own family experience—however little the details of that experience may actually abide our question—then we will find interest in J. H. Padel's recent speculations about the relationship of the sonnets to the death of Shakespeare's son.[8] Whatever the truth may be, it is intriguing that Shakespeare had a brother named Edmund, who also became an actor, and who fathered a bastard son named Edward. This is one of a number of nagging similarities, such as that between the names Hamlet and Hamnet, or between the maiden name of Shakespeare's mother and the forest of Arden where all troubles are healed, or still again the rumor, reported by Rowe, of a gift of a thousand pounds from Southampton to Shakespeare, which Empson thinks must somehow pertain to the thousand pounds owed Falstaff by Prince Hal. These nagging similarities do not constitute evidence, but we are somehow reluctant to put them out of our minds. My visceral feeling is that the presence of Edmund and Edward, brother and bastard, in Shakespeare's familial awareness somehow per-

---

[8] "Shakespeare's Sonnets—Sonnet 146," in *Times* (London) *Literary Supplement*, Oct. 21, 1977.

tains to his creation of Edmund and Edgar, brother and bastard, in his most familial play.

The figure of Edmund stands in starkest tension to the hegemony of the family in the play itself. If we think of the processional entry of Lear and his retainers at the beginning as having some of the formulaic depthlessness of royalty on playing cards, or perhaps even more appropriately as possessing the depthlessness of some grouped and resplendent representation of royal appearances on a late medieval tapestry, then we can think of Edmund as an unwanted thread dangling from that tapestry, a thread that, when tugged at by the play's action, comes out, not alone, but rather begins to unravel the frozen hierarchies of the tapestry itself. The pregnant encounter that opens the play establishes both the frozen hierarchies and the unwanted thread, for there we see two friends, who happen to be earls, exchanging courtesies from their hierarchical security, and one bastard, introduced with unintentional callousness and condescension. The bastard stands outside the haven represented by the family, apparently fully accepting the situation as laid down by his inattentive and carelessly joking father. But when we see the bastard alone, we understand how little those grouped hierarchies actually answer to the structure of human need.

Edmund's pathos lies in his exclusion from significant human attention. Nowhere is this more apparent than in a single line that, standing in the very midst of his plain-dealing villainy, nonetheless reverberates as a universal cry of agony. At the beginning of the second act, having involved Edgar in their father's suspicions, Edmund says, "I hear my father coming" (2.1.29). We pause at Edmund's use of the adjective "my." Edmund next tells Edgar to "draw, seem to defend yourself"; and then, as Edgar flees, Edmund says, "Some blood drawn on me would beget opinion / Of my more fierce endeavor." He next calls out (the words now beginning to reverberate beyond the immediate situation): "Father, father! / Stop, stop! No help?" Gloucester enters, the torches he brings with him ironically prefiguring not only the torch of the foul fiend Flibbertigibbet but also that darkness of the evolving situation in which no torch will avail him. By torchlight he sees nothing: "Now, Edmund, where's the villain?" The deprivation of a lifetime is in Edmund's answer: "Look, sir, I bleed" (2.1.42). But here, as elsewhere, Gloucester looks past his son into the miasma of self-preoccupation: "Where is the villain, Edmund?" is his only answer to the poignant cry. Small wonder, then, when he is blinded in act 4 and the Old Man says, "You cannot see your way," Gloucester's answer seems to be the voice of justice: "I have no way and therefore want no eyes; / I stumbled when I saw" (4.1.17-19).

The pathos of Edmund's "Look, sir, I bleed" constitutes an emotional nadir for the play, and it erupts from the family situation, as does an opposite but complementary emotional zenith: Lear's eulogy of the dead Cordelia: "Her voice was ever soft, / Gentle and low, an excellent thing in woman" (5.3.274-275). The power of the specification lies in its diminuendo of observation contrasted with its crescendo of emotion; but its substance comes from the repeated observations of family interaction, the attention paid to Cordelia by her father. And this attention is starkly opposed to Gloucester's inattention to Edmund.

In largest description, indeed, the opposites that generate the play's moral movement can be viewed as the struggle between attention and inattention ("O, I have ta'en / Too little care of this!"). The truth, both of the play and of human life, is that human inattention destroys the family as haven. But the family as haven, though it undergoes vicissitudes that reveal it to be largely illusion and absolutely so in terms of the insubstantial positings of the play's beginning, complements the idea of a heartless world. The bleakness of the *King Lear* cosmos stands in ironic tension to the posited security of family concern:

> No, I will weep no more. In such a night
> To shut me out! Pour on, I will endure.
> In such a night as this! O Regan, Goneril.
> (3.4.17-19)

The storm that harrows Lear compounds the irony of his familial illusion:

> Rumble thy bellyful. Spit, fire. Spout, rain!
> Nor rain, wind, thunder, fire are my daughters.
> I tax not you, you elements, with unkindness.
> I never gave you kingdom, called you children,
> You owe me no subscription.
>
> (3.2.14-18)

The storm is only the bleakest intensification of the idea of an uncaring cosmos, a heartless world. The play throughout exists in what I have elsewhere called "a nightmare corner of thought."

We may note, finally, that the mighty process by which familial haven is dissipated into heartless world results in the almost inconceivable power of the trial scene in the storm-swept hovel, where the family is virtually turned inside out. The vast dialectical movement of the play's imagery and emotion is from insubstantial something toward and into nothing itself and out again to renewed and substantial something. The insubstantial something is the familial relationships and political and social hierarchies posited at the beginning; the nothing, brought alive by the repeated invocations of the word in the play's fabric of discourse and represented by repeated tropes of divestiture, from shelter to storm, from castle to hovel, from fine raiment to rags to nakedness itself, and, finally, from reason to madness, begins to reemerge as substantial something in the awesome trial scene. There the family situation is reversed. Cordelia is absent, having been replaced by the Fool. Goneril and Regan, the two other members of the family, are on trial on the mad but wonderful familial charge of having "kicked the poor king her father" (3.6.47-48). But Goneril and Regan are actually as "be-noth-inged" as Cordelia, for Goneril is a joint stool, and Regan another, "whose warped looks proclaim / What store her heart is made on."

From this point the often noted wonder ensues. The worldly situation of Lear and Cordelia, except for the momentary calm of their reconciliation, grows worse and worse, but their spiritual situation becomes better and better, until it rises to the transcendent heights of gilded butterflies, purged to the ultimate relationship of "We two alone." All the sources concur in saying that Lear and Cordelia defeated their enemies and that Lear reigned once again over Britain. But in this play we have instead the choric cry of Edgar at the final battle: "King Lear hath lost, he and his daughter ta'en." For worldly success would have worked against Shakespeare's final distillation of human meaning into the heavenly quintessence of family relationship. Father and daughter are more truly family than even husband and wife; and the familial nucleus of "We two alone" persists, in this greatest of Shakespeare's visions, beyond life into death itself.

Six

King Lear and
the Two Abysses

Lawrence Danson

I want to talk about the exigency of *King Lear*. In this I am not alone: commentators repeatedly testify to the special arduousness of the *Lear* experience; no other play provokes as much preliminary flexing of whatever critical, moral, dramaturgical, or poetical muscle we bring to a play as does *King Lear*. The phenomenon is sufficiently intriguing to be worth a moment's glance.

There is, to look no further, the famous case of John Keats, who in a sublimity of procrastination wrote a whole sonnet "On Sitting Down to Read *King Lear* Once Again." It is not the best of Keats's poems (the magnitude of the challenge does not guarantee the quality of the response), but its terms are symptomatic of what many of us feel when we confront the play. Keats bids adieu to the indolent pleasures of "golden tongued Romance,"

> for, once again, the fierce dispute
> Betwixt damnation and impassion'd clay
> Must I burn through; once more humbly assay ‹
> The bitter-sweet of this Shakespearian fruit.

Drama is conflict, of course; but Keats is preparing himself for a titanic struggle not so much between dramatic characters as between two elemental forces: a minimally defined but determined humanity ("impassion'd clay"), on the one hand, and its giant opponent, "damnation," on the other. A fierce dispute, indeed; yet Keats prepares to enter it again, with a strategy suitably complex or oxymoronic: simultaneously he will "burn through" and "humbly assay" this greatest and apparently never-quite-finished dramatic challenge.

Hazlitt's more prosaic testimony is similar, and to me especially endearing. Hazlitt begins by admitting, "We wish that we could pass this play over, and say nothing about it"—a demurrer that surely fulfills the injunction to "speak what we feel, not what we ought to say." But that injunction is in fact what brings on Hazlitt's momentary funk: "All that we can say must fall far short of the subject; or even of what we ourselves conceive of it. To attempt to give a description of the play itself or of its effect upon the mind, is mere impertinence: yet"—says Hazlitt, bravely accepting our necessary inadequacy—"we must say something."[1]

This phenomenon—a confession of inadequacy accompanying a determination to persist in the face of pain and failure—is not only a Romantic one. We recall that Dr. Johnson had to summon all his courage "to read again the last scenes of the play [when he] undertook to revise them as an editor." And in our time too—if my sensations can add anything to the general suffrage—*King Lear* continues to impress us with its unique strenuousness. This tells us something about the play as well as about its commentators—about the way *King Lear* so involves us in its action that reader, audience, actor, or critic may feel, as do the characters in the play, that it will take unusual strength to endure all the play's awful goings hence and comings hither.

Why is *King Lear* a trial, a thing to be endured even in the foreknowledge of failure? The subject matter alone does not fully explain it. However terrible the deaths of Lear and Cordelia may be, they are not more terrible than many other things in or out of Shakespeare. The remarkable thing, and worth exploring, is that they seem terrible at all, for we know little about Cordelia and much that is unpleasant about Lear. Considered in terms of its subject matter alone, the ending of

---

[1] *The Complete Works of William Hazlitt*, ed. P. P. Howe (London: J. M. Dent, 1930), vol. 4, p. 257.

King Lear will not necessarily be the barely endurable thing it was for Dr. Johnson. To the spectacle of the suffering and death of the innocent, responses can be as various as those of the different brothers Karamazov, one of whom was led by that spectacle to the love of God, while another respectfully returned to God his ticket of admission. Freud discovered in the play's final tableau a wish-fulfilling image of mankind's marriage to its forbidden bride, an easeful death. And Freud's romantically consolatory way of enduring the ending of *King Lear* is not really so far from its antecedent Christian consolation, which found in death, as Hamlet did, "a consummation devoutly to be wished." These comments are not intended to dispose of the problems of the play's ending. They are meant simply to indicate that it is worth inquiring further into why many of the play's best commentators have found it nearly unencounterable and never fully recountable—at the same time that they may be prepared to say of this ordeal (as Hazlitt did) that it is "the best of all Shakespear's plays."

The play's size, the impression it gives of sheer bigness, is the most obvious feature, and so a place to begin. *King Lear* exists primarily outdoors, in the unaccommodated world; it stretches to the sea. And at its center is Lear himself, a giant form who dwarfs even the other Shakespearean tragic heroes. Hamlet and Macbeth are more fully articulated; Hamlet, at least, is psychologically more various. But no one, not even Othello or Coriolanus, has Lear's massive musculature. In him duration becomes magnitude; he is so hugely active for so long that finally the most remarkable thing to be said is that he has "borne most: we that are young / Shall never see so much, nor live so long." Lear endures his tough world until he seems less a victim than another aspect of the wind and rain and thunder and spouting hurricanoes in which he hugely exists. And all this bigness in the play's central character demands from us an equally immense sympathetic response. It takes all our energy just to keep up with that awful old man whose demands—on his children, his subjects, nature itself, and on us as audience—are so monstrous and inspiring.

The large scale on which Lear lives has its moral or thematic concomitant. As Lear is not, psychologically, the most various of characters, so the moral situation in his play seems disconcertingly gross. What in other plays would be questions of real import and interest—affixing precise degrees of blame, for instance, or discovering the moral cause before its effects—tends to dwindle in *King Lear*. In all that storm, does it really signify whether Lear was (a) merely old, or (b) exceptionally foolish, or (c) criminally misguided when he undertook the love test and the division of the kingdom? Is Lear, as he claims, a man more sinned against than sinning? Professor McFarland observed that in *Lear* we are beyond the usefulness of the categories of good and evil. In that place for convenience called the heath, where Lear is found "contending with the fretful elements" and striving in "his little world of man to outscorn / The to-and-fro-conflicting wind and rain"—in that exigent place—the questions that would in other plays be necessities may rightly appear to the audience of *King Lear* "but a trifle here."

And yet—"Great thing of us forgot!"—in recalling the overwhelming bigness of *King Lear* it is easy to neglect what seems to me equally important in creating the play's unique sense of arduousness, that is, the whole astonishingly busy world of small things that populate the play's vast spaces. The strenuousness of *King Lear* is found not only in such horrific scene-painting as, for instance, this of Kent's:

> Since I was man,
> Such sheets of fire, such bursts of horrid thunder,
> Such groans of roaring wind and rain, I never
> Remember to have heard. Man's nature cannot carry
> Th' affliction nor the fear.
>
> (3.2.45-49)

Such an assertion of cosmic upheaval would finally be mere bombast were it not that in its midst we, like the characters, must also remember the minutest things, must keep in mind's eye a wretchedly small hovel, imagine "the wren . . . and the small gilded fly," a sampire gatherer and mice-sized fishermen, dogs and lice, a joint stool, an eyeball, a button, a pair of lips, a feather, a breath. Repeatedly the play's language focuses attention, not on the vast, but on the minute particulars, on what Professor Goldman calls the play's histrionic imagery. Lear at one moment bids the "all-shaking thunder, / Strike flat the thick rotundity o' th' world," and at the next remembers a "Poor Fool and knave" and the vile straw that "the art of our necessities" makes precious (3.2.6-7, 69-72). So too for the audience: one of the most interesting ways in which the play imposes its sense of arduousness is by the almost impossible yet necessary act of double focus it requires to peer upward toward that unreachably vast heaven from which the storm comes and downward toward the busy populous world of tiny but distinct forms on which it falls.

The play stretches us "between the two abysses of Infinity and Nothingness." The phrase (translated) is Pascal's, and it appears in a well-known section of Pascal's *Pensées* that seems to me, however historically anomalous, to have a striking relevance to *King Lear*. Typically for him, Pascal here asks us to engage our reason in a way that makes us doubt the sufficiency of that faculty, to use the mind itself until the mind is baffled. He proposes, as I think *King Lear* imposes, an act of double focus: first, Pascal asks man to "contemplate Nature in her full and lofty majesty," directing his gaze upward and outward past sun and stars until the perceiver and indeed "the tiny cell where he lodges, to wit the universe," seem by comparison the merest lost specks in creation. "What," asks Pascal, "is a man face to face with infinity?"[2] Then Pascal asks man to reverse the process, to use, as it were, the microscope instead of the telescope. "Let him seek out the most delicate thing he knows; let a mite present to view, in its tiny body, parts incomparably more tiny, legs with their joints, veins in the legs, blood in the veins, humours in the blood, drops in the humours, vapours in the drops. Subdividing again, let him exhaust himself in these conceptions." The result

---

[2] All quotations are from *Pascal's Pensées*, ed. and trans. H. F. Stewart (New York: Pantheon, 1950), pp. 19-25. I use Stewart's text and arrangement, with his facing page translation, in which I silently make a few very minor stylistic adjustments.

of the optical back-and-forth, this shifting gestalt, is deeply disruptive to our sense of self: "our human body, which a moment ago was imperceptible in our universe, which is itself imperceptible in the sum of things, is now a colossus, nay a world, nay a universe, compared with the nothingness which lies beyond our reach" ("[le] néant où l'on ne peut arriver"). Pascal's purpose is to disrupt and unsettle, finally to exhaust the mind in an impossible effort to discover some resting place for our human self-conception: "If a man will look at himself as I suggest, the sight will terrify him; and, seeing himself suspended in the material form given him by Nature, between the two abysses of Infinity and Nothingness, he will tremble." Considering himself from the two extreme points of view, Pascal's man finds himself "a cypher compared with the Infinite, an All compared with Nothing." It is a terrible fate for Pascal's man to be "equally unable to see the Nothing whence he springs, and the Infinite in which he is swallowed up." He yearns for fixity in a world inimical to his reason's demands: "We have a burning desire to find a sure resting place and a final fixed basis whereon to build a tower rising to the Infinite; but our whole foundation cracks, and the earth yawns to the abyss."

In *King Lear* it is two acts before that abyss opens, but there are intimations from the start. They come, paradoxically at first, in the characters' very efforts to take the measure of things—to size up themselves and others, to fix a sense of proportion in a world soon to lose that comforting sense, and to lose it precisely in the attempt at apparently reasonable mensuration. Gloucester's first line is semantically difficult: "in the the division of the kingdom, it appears not which of the dukes he values most, for equalities are so weighed that curiosity in neither can make choice of either's moiety" (1.1.4-7). But we recognize in it the language of a customary calculus—dividing, weighing, valuing, choosing shares. It serves as prologue to Lear's more terrible act of long division. In a moment Gloucester continues in his apparently reasonable vein: "I have a son, sir, by order of law, some year elder than this, who yet is no dearer in my account" (1.1.19-21).

Gloucester is trying to weigh in a scale of common ounces
(I borrow the language from *Troilus and Cressida*) the past
proportion of what, shortly, the play will reveal as the un-
measurable heights and depths of the human heart. All this
attempt at emotional precision, whether in the matter of the
king's choice or of his own family affairs, is taking place
"within a foot / Of th' extreme verge." Once we are over that
edge and find ourselves suspended between the two abysses
of infinity and nothingness, the calm reliance on the old instruments of measurement will seem, not reasonable, but a
symptom of that lost proportion the play dramatizes as insanity.

Inevitably characters will go on measuring, acting as though
there were firm ground on which to establish their instruments: as Pascal knew, mankind cannot bear very much of
a proportionless reality. It is not only the callous sisters who
will weigh things, reckoning, for instance, the need for fifty,
twenty-five, ten, five, or one. Even the good Edgar, at the very
end, is found trying to make things balance out: "The dark
and vicious place where thee he got / Cost him his eyes"
(5.3.174-175). And though Edgar may be right, or possibly
not (as I said, the play treats some great questions with in-
souciance), Edgar's confidence in his ability to balance may
trouble us in light of the play's full experience.

From Gloucester we move to Lear and the results of his
emotional calculation: "Which of you shall we say doth love
us most?" (1.1.51). Goneril's response to this is in various
ways vacuous:

> Sir, I love you more than word can wield the matter;
> Dearer than eyesight, space, and liberty;
> Beyond what can be valued.
>
> (1.1.55-57)

Easily she slides past measurement—"more," "beyond,"
"dearer"; her emotionally facile language presages the va-
cancy that will open inescapably for Lear and for us. But Lear
thinks he hears the silence of those spaces, not in Goneril's
or Regan's language, but in Cordelia's:

LEAR. Nothing?
CORDELIA. Nothing.
LEAR. Nothing will come of nothing. Speak again.
$$(1.1.88\text{-}90)$$

And indeed she does speak, though her coolly measured response is almost lost after the more reverberant "nothings": "I love your majesty / According to my bond, no more nor less." This reply has troubled other admirers of Cordelia besides her father—commentators like Coleridge, for instance, who acknowledged in Cordelia "some little faulty admixture of pride and sullenness." What are we to make of her apparent return to the language of calculation that is proving useless or worse? Or of Kent's similar language when, like Cordelia, he enumerates the bonds (to use Cordelia's fraught word) that tie him to Lear:

> Royal Lear,
> Whom I have ever honored as my king,
> Loved as my father, as my master followed,
> As my great patron thought on in my prayers—
> $$(1.1.139\text{-}142)$$

We may say that, if there is an apparent coldness in Cordelia and Kent, it is only the coldness of truth and precision; that in appealing to their bonds they are trying to establish saving coordinates on an otherwise blank map, trying to domesticate the empty space glimpsed in Goneril's response. But there is more to it, I think, than that, and here we may recall that Pascal was, among other things, a mathematician: sources tell us that he invented a digital calculator, pioneered the theory of probability, and explored the problem of infinitely small numbers. But he was in mathematics as in theology a Pyrrhonist, exploring the limits of reason in order to make us accept the mystery that lies beyond reason. His was a Jansenist calculus, which could bring him to an "O altitudo" at the unfathomableness of God's ways. The attempts by Cordelia and Kent to measure their love for Lear are more like Pascal's calculations than they are like Goneril's or Regan's, or even

Gloucester's emotional arithmetic: they are less an attempt to set limits on love than, by confrontation, to reveal how far those limits are from reason's grasp.

And indeed it is the play's tragic teleology that all the answers can only further precipitate Lear onto his stormy heath. In one confused gesture Lear makes some effort to maintain his old precarious sense of proportion:

> Our self, by monthly course,
> With reservation of an hundred knights,
> By you to be sustained, shall our abode
> Make with you by due turn—

at the same time that he continues, willy-nilly, to annul it: "The sway, / revènue, execution . . . be yours" (1.1.132-138). As the train of knights is divided and subtracted from Lear— the whole business is dramatically astounding for its inexorable pettiness: "What need you five-and-twenty? ten? or five? / . . . What need one?" (2.4.258, 260)—as the tragic work of stripping away begins with a vengeance, Lear discovers the self-destroying terror of seeing himself as Pascal dares us to do, alternately and with equal truth a colossus and a lost speck, merely "unaccommodated man." Lear asks the disguised Kent, "Dost thou know me, fellow?"

> KENT. No, sir, but you have that in your countenance
> which I would fain call master.
> LEAR. What's that?
> KENT. Authority.
>
> (1.4.27-31)

But a moment later, to the same question, "Who am I, sir?" Oswald answers with equal plausibility, "My lady's father" (1.4.78-80). In the Fool's still rougher formulation, Lear has "pared [his] wit o' both sides and left nothing i' th' middle" (1.4.188-189).

Others are experiencing the loss of proportion and place. France is perplexed that Cordelia, who "even but now was [Lear's] best object," has so fallen in price to this "little seeming substance" (1.1.214, 198). France's role in the play is brief but important; he recognizes, as Burgundy cannot, that a new way of taking the measure of things is becoming necessary. Because there is apparently no fixed star by which to take Cordelia's height, France introduces into the play's rhetorical world a language of paradox that will be necessary as it tries to negotiate the abysses of infinity and nothingness:

> Fairest Cordelia, that art most rich being poor,
> Most choice forsaken, and most loved despised. . . .
> . . . .
> Not all the dukes of wat'rish Burgundy
> Can buy this unprized precious maid of me.
> Bid them farewell, Cordelia, though unkind.
> Thou losest here, a better where to find.
>   (1.1.250-261)

To measure the new state of things France employs the proportions of paradox—the paradox of divine reversals, in which the poor become rich, the outcast and despised the first chosen. But France's language, by that token, is still one of extremes; it recognizes polarities but no mean.

Of the play's two simultaneous movements, toward the nothing whence we spring and the infinite in which we are swallowed up, the rhetoric of the latter—the large language that gestures toward infinity—is the more strident, more obvious. We hear it first in Lear's regal presumptuousness and later, ironically, in the terrible curses and invocations that follow from Lear's discovery that he was not everything, that he was not ague-proof. But it is the other movement, the endless falling toward what Pascal calls "[le] néant où l'on ne peut arriver," that seems to me the more interesting. I have already suggested that the play's language of cosmic upheaval might sound merely blustering were it not for the persistent counterpoint of a vividly realized language of small things. The play's madmen and fools and outcasts especially bring with them this counterpoint to the play's vast gestures toward the heavens. From Poor Tom we hear of "pins, wooden pricks, nails, sprigs of rosemary," of "low farms, / Poor pelting villages, sheepcotes, and mills" (2.3.16-18). Poor Tom and the

Fool—and then, with the essential twist of tragic irony, the mad king himself—share this rhetorical function of keeping the play's world populated with a seemingly endless profusion of trifles that prevent us from settling, however uncomfortably, in the large scale summoned by the storm itself and by Lear's cosmic curses. Initially in his rage Lear's attention turns outward and upward to the heavens, high judging Jove, cataracts and hurricanoes and sulphurous and thought-executing fires; but the impression of terrible arduousness comes not alone from that scale but rather from its constant interaction with the other, microscopic scale that descends to snails, oysters, crab apples, eggs, ants, noses, codpieces, eels, a knife, a pillow, a halter in a pew, ratsbane in porridge, curled hair, gloves in a cap, hog, fox, wolf, dog, rustling silks, plackets, pens. Pascal writes that "it needs quite as great capacity to attain the Nothing as the All. . . . The one depends on the other." Madman and fool, natives of the hovel and the ditch, by what they say and by what they are—"The thing itself, unaccommodated man"—conduct the mind toward the abyss of nothingness. And this is one of the most taxing aspects of *King Lear*, this spectacle of its people straining toward "the nothingness that lies beyond our reach."

The spectacle is first and most vividly present in the exchange of that very word, "nothing," between Lear and Cordelia—an exchange soon to be repeated, in diminuendo, between Lear and Lear's shadow, the Fool:

FOOL. Can you make no use of nothing, nuncle?
LEAR. Why, no, boy. Nothing can be made out of nothing.
(1.4.132-135)

Lear's confidence that he knows the value of nothing, and that he can safely distinguish it from the all, is mocked even by the speakers' physical presence: the great father-king and the "little-seeming" daughter of scene one become, in one of the play's many perspectival tricks, the "very foolish fond old man" who needs to be dressed and gently wakened and forgiven by the woman who, like a soul in bliss, seems to tower over him in act 4, scene 7. Our understanding of the one image depends upon the other.

Edgar is the conductor toward the play's promised "nothing"—a difficult and unrewarding role partly because of the exhausting unattainability of that state of perfect vacuity. Edgar's first motion toward it is precipitous; it has often been noticed that there is something excessive in his descent from being, as the title page of the first quarto carefully designates him, "son and heir to the Earl of Gloucester," to being "the basest and most poorest shape / That ever penury, in contempt of man, / Brought near to beast" (2.3.7-9). For purposes of disguise something short of that superlative degree of abjectness would have done. A quest for stability, I suggest, is one motive for the excessiveness of Edgar's disguise: more comforting than the sight of oneself suspended between the two abysses is, as Edgar puts it, "To be worst, / The lowest and most dejected thing of fortune" (4.1.2-3). Edgar begins his descent with a curiously modular statement of negative identity: "Edgar I nothing am" (2.3.21). But the statement is too optimistic; the "I am" frustrates the intention of being "nothing" and keeps Edgar still suspended. For all the precipitousness of this *casus viri illustrius*, Edgar has not fallen far enough; and he will be repeatedly frustrated in his attempt to reach some depth, however awful, that will no longer shift beneath him to reveal still greater depths. It is this endlessly descending motion of *King Lear* that Gerard Manley Hopkins recalls in the sonnet,

> No worst, there is none. Pitched past pitch of grief,
> More pangs will, schooled at forepangs, wilder wring.
> Comforter, where, where is your comforting?
> . . . .
> O the mind, mind has mountains; cliffs of fall
> Frightful, sheer, no-man-fathomed. Hold them cheap
> May who ne'er hung there.

Even as Edgar embraces the "unsubstantial air," because "the wretch that thou hast blown unto the worst / Owes nothing to thy blasts" (4.1.7-9), Gloucester enters the scene, eyeless and in despair, showing Edgar that "worse I may be yet: the worst is not / So long as we can say, 'This is the worst' " (4.1.27-28).

"No worst, there is none": the nothings of *King Lear* always contain less than one had imagined. The bottom shifts again for Edgar; his father's entrance brings with it knowledge of "a cliff whose high and bending head / Looks fearfully in the confinèd deep" (4.1.73-74). In that image the personified cliff bends to look into the depths—the new depths of which, a moment before, Edgar had been unaware. And now there is a new height to be climbed as Gloucester in his turn seeks some final resting place. These emotional and optical shifts are dizzying; they are, as in Pascal's experiment, terrifying.

In act 4, scene 6, at a place domesticated by editors into "Fields near Dover," Edgar and Gloucester (and we with them) undertake, in a startling and dramatic way, a variation on Pascal's experiment with shifting perspectives. I have already referred to Gloucester's early and easy confidence in his own sense of proportion; it is a confidence ironically reflected in that strange exchange with Edmund, when Edmund pretends to hide an ostensibly incriminating note from Edgar. The note, says Edmund, is "Nothing, my lord." Yet Gloucester demands to see this fictive nothing: "The quality of nothing hath not such need to hide itself. Let's see. Come, if it be nothing, I shall not need spectacles" (1.2.31-35). By act 4, truly beyond the need for spectacles, Gloucester can say he knows more now. He has already begun, with a vengeance, his schooling in the nature of Pascalian space. In the storm Gloucester has had his vision trained downward to the diminishing scale: he has seen in Poor Tom the basest and most poorest shape. Meeting now this "Madman and beggar too," he remembers,

I' th' last night's storm I such a fellow saw,
Which made me think a man a worm. My son
Came then into my mind, and yet my mind
Was then scarce friends with him. I have heard more since.
As flies to wanton boys, are we to th' gods,

They kill us for their sport.

(4.1.32-37)

From man to worm, from gods to boys to flies: overwhelmed by this new, disproportionate sense of littleness in relation to the infinite, Gloucester would desperately hurl downward, to embrace finally the elusive "quality of nothing."

The despair that brings Gloucester to his Dover cliffs is the product of his confrontation with life's littleness. Edgar is reciprocally disproportionate in his insistence on the scale of the infinite. When Gloucester, having stepped beyond the extreme verge, awakes from his brief sleep of death, he wants to know, "But have I fall'n, or no?" (4.6.56)—not a bad question, and one the audience may also be asking. Edgar has reassured him: "Ten masts at each make not the altitude / Which thou hast perpendicularly fell: / Thy life's a miracle" (4.6.53-55). But where then is that perfect nothingness toward which the old man thought he was plummeting? As in the Pascalian experiment, the descent reveals the unreachable. One of the significant pictures presented in this odd scene of double focus is that of man's state in a Pascalian universe, a state of suspension and exhausting "in-betweenness," neither on Edgar's heights nor at Gloucester's depths. Edgar bids his blind father, "Look up a-height"—*up*, where (strangely) he would see a sight finally indistinguishable from that seen by one looking *down* "from the dread summit of this chalky bourn": "the shrill-gorged lark so far / Cannot be seen or heard." Up or down, the vision is swallowed in immensity.

In his description of the cliff, Edgar creates a height. This fictive cliff is as much present as anything else in the fiction of *King Lear*; and at the end of the scene we are at the bottom of that cliff. Simultaneously, we are at scene's end where we were at its beginning, on the level plain of the great Globe's stage. Edgar, therefore, is not wrong to assume a truth in the first picture and to reach the Christian conclusion that Gloucester's life is a miracle. Others, though, are no more wrong to see here a pious fraud that cannot prove the heavens are just. And to these ostensible opposites a third alternative must be added—the one that shows man, despite all our Edgar-like graspings toward infinity or our Gloucester-like descents toward nothing, still (while we are in this life) suspended, incapable of reaching either secure extreme. "Let us then," says Pascal, "cease to look for security and stability. Our reason is ever cheated by misleading appearances: nothing can fix the finite between the two Infinities which enclose it and fly from it."

Of Edgar's description of the cliff—"How fearful / And dizzy 'tis to cast one's eyes so low!"—Dr. Johnson objected that "the enumeration of the choughs and crows, the samphire-man and the fishers, counteracts the great effect of the prospect, as it peoples the desert of intermediate vacuity, and stops the mind in the rapidity of its descent through emptiness and horror."[3] But this peopling "the desert of intermediate vacuity" is exactly what is intended: the observed particulars of the scene keep us from the comfort both of Edgar's height and of Gloucester's terminal nothingness. And in the scenes of Lear's madness too (to return now, by way of conclusion, from the so-called subplot to the so-called main plot), we find a world extraordinarily busy with the minutiae of life, some of it appallingly ugly, some poignant. When first we meet Lear striving "in his little world of man to outscorn / The to-and-fro-conflicting wind and rain" (3.1.10-11), we find immediately in his speeches the interdependence of the all and nothing, that double focus, that helps impart to the play its sense of terrible arduousness. "Blow, winds, and crack your cheeks. Rage, blow!" But the fully apocalyptic nature of Lear's rage is realized only when he glances from the top to the bottom, descending to the unseen sources or seeds of life: "Strike flat the thick rotundity o' th' world, / Crack Nature's molds, all germains spill at once, / That makes ingrateful man" (3.2.7-9).

The Fool plays his part in this, bringing us back from Lear's spitting fires and high-engendered battles to his own scale of

---

[3] *Johnson on Shakespeare*, ed. Arthur Sherbo, Yale Edition of the Works of Samuel Johnson, vols. 7-8 (New Haven: Yale Univ. Press, 1968), p. 695.

heads and houses and codpieces, to a toe and a corn on a toe and a fair woman making mouths in a glass. But Lear is becoming his own fool; his own speech becomes busy with quick little satirical vignettes and fragments of human form. For all the "dreadful pudder o'er our heads," Lear, learning a new way of looking, finds out the gods' enemies:

> Tremble, thou wretch,
> That hast within thee undivulgèd crimes
> Unwhipped of justice. Hide thee, thou bloody hand,
> Thou perjured, and thou simular of virtue
> That art incestuous.

> (3.2.51-55)

Lear's anatomizing madness (act 4, scene 6) finds lechery in the wren and fly, authority's image in the cur; it sees the pygmy's piercing straw, the accuser's lips and the scurvy politician's glass eyes. These vivid images and grotesque metonymies have their counterparts in other dramas of the period: they recall the speeches of satirical disgust lavishly indulged in by the Bosolas, Malevoles, Vindices, or Bussys of Jacobean tragedy. But in *Lear* they do not seem intrusive; rather, they seem an authentic psychological response to the *Lear* situation. And this is so, in part, because the observation of these forms, however loathsome, is a psychologically necessary rebound from the vastness of one scale of seeing to the intense particularity of the other. So too with the other things Lear has taken too little care of—the "poor naked wretches" with their "houseless heads and unfed sides, / [Their] looped and windowed raggedness" (3.4.28-31). Considering well the thing itself, unaccommodated man, is one way of attempting to fix some finite in the eternal to-and-fro between infinity and nothingness.

But the proportion-giving forms become still further fragmented by Lear's madness; they become themselves indistinguishable in all that psychic immensity. And this brings us to the question of the play's final exigency. In their scene of reconciliation, Lear thinks he has caught Cordelia. Joyfully he would be away with her to prison to "sing like birds i' th' cage," for now he has a vision of them unchangeably among

"God's spies" (or, in Johnson's gloss on that phrase, "angels commissioned to survey and report on the lives of men")—a transcendent vantage point indeed. But from the moment of Lear's reentrance bearing the dead Cordelia we are forced again to confront the two abysses. From the rhetoric of the vast—"Had I your tongues and eyes, I'd use them so / That heaven's vault should crack"—Lear's attention turns to "a looking-glass; / If that her breath will mist or stain the stone, / Why, then, she lives." Kent wonders, "Is this the promised end?"—and from that intimation of a universal doom we are wrenched to "This feather stirs." There is in these final moments a terrible strain—the strain of hope against hope, as well as an actual physical strain—as Lear bends to see what cannot be seen: Cordelia's breath; to hear what cannot be heard: her voice that was ever soft, gentle, and low and that now pronounces nothing. A last time Lear's consciousness flashes out and down toward those characteristic images: "Why should a dog, a horse, a rat, have life, / And thou no breath at all?" before again facing vacuity: "Thou'lt come no more, / Never, never, never, never, never."

In Lear's last moment the dependency of the infinitely great upon the infinitely small is most forcefully communicated. "Do you see this?" Lear asks, demanding that we strain the senses further: "Look on her. Look, her lips, / Look there, look there." But what are we to see? No two commentators will ever fully agree about this most daringly indeterminate of dramatic conclusions. Lear's demand that we look and see forces us back upon our own sense of things, our sense of what the sight of an innocent dead young woman's lips tells us about the universe in which she and we have dwelt. I will not repeat the range of possibilities, from bleakest despair or nihilism to the most defiant optimism. It is more important for my purpose to notice that, by the nature of the play's experience, which has shown us man in the form given him by nature, suspended between the two abysses of infinity and nothingness, whatever we believe we see there, whether it is a modernist nothing or a Jansenist all, we believe it by virtue of a strenuous leap of faith.

Seven

"Nothing Almost Sees Miracles": Tragic Knowledge in *King Lear*

Thomas P. Roche, Jr.

I will begin by agreeing with Professor Danson about the perplexing ambiguities of Lear's death vision: "Look on her. Look, her lips, / Look there, look there." The problem is what Lear means and what Shakespeare wants us to see about Lear's vision, and, as Professor Danson suggested, the answers are legion. But the interpretation of this line is crucial to our understanding of the play: as Lear's last words they stand as his latest understanding of what he has experienced and by implication what his kingdom and we as audience have learned from that experience.

Before I attend to what I see as the meaning of that crucial last line, I would like to explain the reason I chose this title for my lecture. The title is derived from a speech by Kent in act 2, scene 2. The faithful Kent has been put in the stocks, and at the end of the scene he is left alone to comment on his situation:

> Good king, that must approve the common saw,
> Thou out of heaven's benediction com'st
> To the warm sun.
> Approach, thou beacon to this under globe,
> That by thy comfortable beams I may
> Peruse this letter. Nothing almost sees miracles
> But misery. I know 'tis from Cordelia,

Who hath most fortunately been informed
Of my obscurèd course. And shall find time
From this enormous state, seeking to give
Losses their remedies. All weary and o'erwatched,
Take vantage, heavy eyes, not to behold
This shameful lodging. Fortune, good night;
Smile once more, turn thy wheel.

(2.2.163-176)

It is a very strange speech from the point of view of sense, syntax, and dramatic function. It is one of those speeches in which we hear about the numerous letters dispatched or received, which in other plays would be part of the exposition, that is, devices to alert the audience to information they should know to understand the action. But in this play this device of exposition is used to keep the characters informed of plot developments that we as the audience see before us center stage. The exposition value of this particular letter is unusually elusive. We must assume that Kent has had it with him throughout the whole scene and that his invocation of the sun to let him read it at this point is to inform us that it is now night, which we already knew from the previous action of the scene. In any case Kent already knows what is in the letter.

None of these realistic assessments of the speech in its context will help us with the profoundly enigmatic nature of the sentence that comes between Kent's desire to read the letter and his acknowledgment that he knows already that the letter is from Cordelia and what its contents are. The line is: "Nothing almost sees miracles / But misery." One modern edition defers to Kittredge's paraphrase of the line: "for when we are in despair, any relief seems miraculous," a paraphrase that I hope will allow me to say something more about the possibilities inherent in the words. The difficulties occur mainly with the possibile relationships between the word "almost" and the phrase "but misery." Where and how do they work into the meaning of the sentence? Is it

Nothing   almost sees miracles
or   Nothing almost   sees miracles

137

The tautology of the first reading, a total negation, has already been defused by Cordelia's "nothing" and Lear's redundant reply "Nothing will come of nothing, speak again." Even at this point in the play we know that nothing is more than nothing. But even if we accept this contextual adjudication, we are faced with the further problem of what it is almost to see miracles and how this gropingly potential vision is related to the phrase "but misery." In short, how are we to assess the alliterative connection between "miracles" and "misery"? Are they to be equated or opposed? Are we to understand that

> Nothing   almost sees miracles but really sees misery
> or   Nothing but misery   almost sees miracles

In either case, what does it do for us except as we readers or spectators wish to see either miracles or misery? Even then there may be nothing.

We might take the second possibility of "almost" modifying "nothing," in the sense of "almost nothing," which at least qualifies the total negation of the first option to the logical possibility of some members of the class of nothing being able to perform the act of seeing miracles. But once more the qualifying phrase "but misery" complicates. Are we to understand

> Almost nothing   sees miracles but really sees misery
> or   Almost nothing but misery   sees miracles

I will not continue to tease the possibilities of this line because in production it slips by virtually unnoticed in the context of its speech. Nonetheless, the richness of its ambiguities runs the gamut from worried optimism (almost nothing but misery sees miracles) to cynical nihilism (nothing almost sees miracles but really sees misery). The sentence becomes almost a paradigm of the various ways of interpreting the play, from a Lear transcending his misery into a miracle beyond our ken to a Lear descending into a further misery that deludes him as a miracle. Nothing in Kent's speech or in Kent's character will help us to outwit the possibilities of the line, to assess its significance in the total action of the play, or to avoid the polishing of our close-reading instincts.

I have used this line as my title because the problems it presents us as readers are the same as those from Lear's last lines, though the latter cannot be tormented as easily with the aid of grammar or syntax. There is one major difference between the two lines: Shakespeare could allow Kent's line to expend itself in ambiguity, but he could not allow the same lack of restraint to Lear's.

"Look on her. Look, her lips, / Look there, look there." The stage action is being directed by Lear to the lips of his dead daughter. Surely Shakespeare wanted this last directorial gesture of Lear to recall his first definitive error of vision when he mistook the word "nothing" as the embodiment of a human response. Whatever our interpretation of Lear's vision, I think we must all agree that once more in a truer sense Cordelia is saying "nothing." Even the audience knows when one is dead. I think that Danson was right when he said that we bring with us our own set of values to assess the play, but I cannot accept the relativism of that position. I do not think that Shakespeare was out to accommodate all of our ideas in his play, that he probably had some meaning in his mind when he wrote those enigmatic lines, some meaning that would accommodate the whole action of the play and not just the plangent image of an ancient man speaking to the dead body of a daughter he had loved and misunderstood.

No critic of the play wants to dispose of Lear's last lines as anything but crucial, but the explanation of those lines has convinced me that the explications are not so much a reading of the lines as a telling of beliefs, the world view of the critic. My old teacher and colleague, Richard Blackmur, stated the problem succinctly when he wrote: "We now look to Shakespeare to see what has happened to us; and that is naturally a hard job to find out."[1] There is an inescapable rereading of

[1] R. P. Blackmur, *Anni Mirabiles 1921-1925: Reason in the Madness of Literature, Four Lectures Presented under the Auspices of the Gertrude Clarke Whittal Poetry and Literature Fund* (Washington, D.C.: Library of Congress, 1956), p. 55. The whole passage reads: "But it may possibly be

Shakespeare in every age, else why would he have been "not of an age but for all time," as Ben Jonson assured us. I am not for a moment suggesting that we reject Ben Jonson's or Sam Johnson's readings of Shakespeare, or Coleridge's, Bradley's, Granville-Barker's, or Frye's. But I do suggest that these meanings may not reflect Shakespeare's intention, that there is still room to sort out the less valuable readings and to continue as best and humbly as we may to reconstruct a historical matrix within which the plays might exist intellectually and that will force out what is merely our own imposition of meaning on the plays in our attempt to see what has become of us. I do not intend a witch hunt of heretics or an archaeological reconstruction. Rather, I want to concentrate on one aspect of interpreting *Lear* and the other major tragedies in the twentieth century, and that is the problem of tragic knowledge.

In its simplest form tragic knowledge is a set of critical assumptions about the triumph of the tragic hero in defeat. It posits that a tragic hero attains a kind of knowledge that redeems him, his suffering, and reconciles his claims to the world he leaves impoverished for his loss. It is an attractive theory because it allows each viewer or reader to let the hero off on whatever grounds he chooses, granting to the hero

---

that those of us are right who believe that both the nature of literature and the nature of the audience have changed from previous times. The literature has become more inaccesible and the audience more illiterate; I mean, of course, that Shakespeare has become more inaccessible than previously to the audience presumed to want to use him. I mean also that Shakespeare is now open to uses to which he would not previously have been put. Shakespeare has changed: anyway our consciousness of him has changed, it matters nothing which way this is put. We now look to Shakespeare to see what has happened to us; and that is naturally a hard job to find out. The change is only superficial; it is only that we are able to take less for granted than our ancestors were; it is only that we do not have nearly so adequate a set of conventions as they. We have invented so many ways of formularizing consciously what we know that it sometimes seems we know, by nature, nothing at all. We are as bad off as Socrates complaining about the specialization of knowledge at Athens in his time; by which I do not mean to be frivolous but only to suggest that the availability of our knowledge depends deeply on the attitude we take towards it."

whatever knowledge the critic brings to the play. It posits not only that the hero attains such knowledge but also that the hero has the total sympathy of the audience and that his final acquisition of this tragic knowledge is the "chance which does redeem all sorrows." This chance of tragic knowledge bothers me because no critic has ever convinced me that such knowledge ever comes to any Shakespearean hero. I suppose that the simplest case for the twentieth century is Marlowe's *Doctor Faustus*, in which the hero is encased not only within his hellish overreaching but also within a clearly defined sixteenth-century Christian context that encompasses both the hero and the hellish allurement. To speak of heroism or of tragic knowledge within the context of this play is to deny historical realities too patently provable by text and context to require refutation except for those who want to fill Faustus's chair and earn damnation. If one wanted a chair and did not believe in damnation, one might make Faustus into a kind of pre-Blakean Satan, who jogged all over Europe, but it would be hard to prove this point to me unless Marlowe had gone on to write *Doctor Faustus II* as he did with *Tamburlaine*. I do not suppose that Harry Levin would agree with me, but that is part of the point I am making.

To return to Shakespeare, I suppose that Macbeth comes as close to tragic knowledge as any of the major tragic heroes. He has gone wrong. I can think of no critic who has argued that the killing of Duncan is in any way good. Macbeth's simultaneous rise and decline, with his gradual recognition of the enormity of the act he has committed, brings him, in the lies he has to tell himself, to the final rejection of witches, prophecies, ambition.

> And be these juggling fiends no more believed,
> That palter with us in a double sense;
> That keep the word of promise to our ear,
> And break it to our hope. I'll not fight with thee.
> (5.8.19-22)

Are we to suppose that his understanding that he has misinterpreted all the omens given him (when he already knows that he has transgressed all the definitions of what man is, "who would do more is none") leads him to a knowledge that we should embrace as salutary or helpful to that human condition we piously call for in our criticism? What kind of heroism is:

> Lay on, Macduff;
> And damned be him that first cries, "Hold, enough!"
> (5.8.33-34)

What knowledge has been won: that he has lost, that he can still persist until defeated into death? What heroism there? One wonders how King James viewed the play, but I do not wonder too long because I read the play as a moral and metaphysical indictment of Macbeth's actions. We could quibble about the nature of heroism in defeat, but in *Macbeth* there can be no question about moral proprieties. Do we really want to argue that Macbeth's overreaching even to death is the heroic quality with which we want to identify in the play? Is that what the play is about?

Macbeth is an easy example because no critic would want to deny that he has done wrong, but when we come to the other tragic heroes of Shakespeare, we are in murkier waters. Few in the twentieth century want to question the morality of a young prince, a wife slayer, and a crazy old man. They are heroes, but here I must restrict myself to the subject of their tragic knowledge.[2] Hamlet's knowledge is that he is dying and has been forgiven by Laertes, but his main concern is not his deeds but his reputation: "report me and my cause aright / To the unsatisfied." A second time he must implore Horatio:

> O God, Horatio, what a wounded name,
> Things standing thus unknown, shall live behind me!
> If thou didst ever hold me in thy heart,
> Absent thee from felicity awhile,

---

[2] Our modern conception of a literary hero came very late. *The Oxford English Dictionary* cites Dryden (1697) as the first usage. The term "hero" in the sixteenth century was generally restricted to semidivine creatures like Achilles.

And in this harsh world draw thy breath in pain,
To tell my story.   *A march afar off.*
                    What warlike noise is this?
                            (5.2.346-351)

It is, of course, the very story that has been the three hours'
traffic of our stage. None of the problems that have haunted
Hamlet throughout the play has been solved, except through
death, the wiping out of two families and one kingdom. "My
story," that superlative self-interest in narrative craft, that
overweening sense of self, is superseded by that sudden question at the end of the speech: "What warlike noise is this?"
Hamlet has either ignored or denigrated the actions of Fortinbras, but here, in this penultimate speech, he is forced to
take cognizance of another force, soon to impinge on his story
and to take the kingdom that would have been his. The warlike
noise, the play tells us, is Fortinbras's salute to the English
ambassadors, who have come to announce the deaths of Rosencrantz and Guildenstern—needless deaths, needless em-
bassy. The speech of the ambassador and all but the last speech
of Fortinbras are usually submerged in the attempt to make
Hamlet's last speech important, definitive. "The rest is silence"
is the kind of ambiguity that appeals to the twentieth-century
readers of Shakespeare's plays. Language and politics are un-
important except as they apply to individuals; only Hamlet,
the hero, is triumphant in his total defeat, and his tragic
knowledge is: "What warlike noise is this?" This is a sudden
eruption of issues that Hamlet has ignored throughout the
play. Whatever one thinks of Rosencrantz's and Guildenstern's action in the play, Hamlet's dismissal of them, "not
shriving time allowed," is as malicious an act as sparing
Claudius only to catch him in some act "that his soul may be
as damned and black as hell." I see no way to excuse Hamlet
for either of these acts; it is malice, pure and simple. Fortinbras, whose apparently futile war to restore his father's lands
is badly misinterpreted by Hamlet, enters at this point in the
play and speaks. It is he (not Horatio) who gives the final
praise to Hamlet, and his praise is to Hamlet the prince and

143

soldier that he never was. He can afford to praise him, because, "dying voice" or not, the kingdom has come into his hands, as Cavafy's ironic poem, "King Claudius," suggests:

> Later, once the kingdom had calmed down
> and the king was lying in his grave—
> he was killed by his nephew, the prince,
> who never went to England
> but escaped from the ship on his way there—
> a certain Horatio came forward
> and tried to exonerate the prince
> by telling some stories of his own.
> He said that the voyage to England
> had been a secret plot, and orders
> had been given to kill the prince there
> (but this was never clearly ascertained).
> He also spoke of poisoned wine—
> wine poisoned by the king.
> It's true that Laertes spoke of this too.
> But couldn't he have been lying?
> Couldn't he have been mistaken?
>
> And when did he say all this?
> While dying of his wounds, his mind reeling,
> his talk seemingly delirious.
> As for the poisoned weapons,
> it was shown later that the poisoning
> hadn't been done by the king at all:
> Laertes himself had done it.
> But Horatio, whenever pressed,
> would produce even the ghost as a witness:
> the ghost said this and that,
> the ghost did this and that!
>
> Because of all this, though letting Horatio talk,
> most people in their hearts
> pitied the poor king,
> who, with all these ghosts and fairy tales,
> was unjustly killed and disposed of.

Yet Fortinbras, who profited
by winning the throne so easily,
gave full attention and weight
to every world Horatio said.[3]

Although I am not yet of Eliot's party in thinking that
Othello is merely cheering himself up in the "Soft you, a word
or two before you go" speech, I am more than a little bothered
by Othello's description of himself as "one that loved not
wisely but too well." How can one love too well without
perverting the meaning of the word into a callous self-esteem
that ignores that dead body on the bed? What kind of knowledge does Othello achieve? The question is complicated by
the textual crux of that speech. If Othello is the base Indian
who threw away a pearl richer than all his tribe, then he is
still within the restricting self-justifications of loving not wisely
but too well. If he is the base Judean, that is, if he sees himself
as Judas, then he sees himself as one who has betrayed. He
is a traitor to mankind and to the bond he swore to Desdemona. If this latter reading is correct, then Othello's last
speech is plainly an act of despair,[4] and not an act of knowledge that justifies his killing of Desdemona and of himself.

> I kissed thee ere I killed thee. No way but this,
> Killing myself, to die upon a kiss.
>
> (5.2.357-358)

If Othello is referring to Judas, this kiss can only recall the
kiss of welcome that Judas gives Christ before his betrayal in
the garden. If that allusion is intended, what are we to think
of the dying kiss, surely of no comfort to the dead Desdemona?
For Othello, is it expiating knowledge, or merely a dramatic
act of making gestures in the face of despair? What are we
to make of his acts and his words? In what sense can they be
called heroic or knowledgeable? Surely if there is such a thing

---

[3] C. P. Cavafy, *Collected Poems*, trans. Edmund Keeley and Philip Sherrard,
ed. George Savidis (Princeton: Princeton Univ. Press, 1975), pp. 339-343.

[4] On the last speech of Othello see Joan Ozark Holmer, "Othello's Threnos:
'Arabian Trees' and 'Indian' versus 'Judean'," *Shakespeare Studies*, 13
(1980), 145-167.

as tragic knowledge, that knowledge must make sense of the acts committed within the context of the world that the audience normally inhabits. I think it would be a great error to assume that that context did not include the broad and comprehensive general truths of Christianity as they were presented throughout the Middle Ages and Renaissance as dogma, as image, as truth. Because we have unlearned that truth as dogma and forgotten it as image, we are in danger of misreading the images.

I originally thought I might trace the development of the theory of tragic knowledge during this lecture, but that turned out to be too great a task for the time available. I can say that the concept does not appear in Aristotle, certainly not in the Middle Ages, and not in the seventeenth-century commentaries on Shakespeare or tragedy. The concept smacks distinctly of an era that wanted to make a real distinction between the suffering individual and the social and political institutions of which he is a part. The concept has its origins somewhere between the time of the dissolution of the belief in providential order in the seventeenth century and the triumph of the individual over the oppressions of a world order that was bequeathed to us by the Romantic revolution. We find hints of the concept in Hegel and in A. C. Bradley. And if the progression from the philosopher to the literary critic suggests a literary preoccupation with the problem, an attempt to divorce common morality from the concerns of literary perception, an attempt to establish literature as a secular replacement for religion, then I think it will be no surprise that that most chameleon of Romantic poets, William Butler Yeats, has produced the most full-fledged version of the concept in "Lapis Lazuli," his late poetic rendition of Keats's "Ode on a Grecian Urn." I mention Yeats's poem, not because it settles any problems of intellectual history, but because it is taught so often in the curriculum of universities that the concept of tragic joy it enunciates has become a cliché in discussions of tragedy.

> All perform their tragic play,
> There struts Hamlet, there is Lear,

That's Ophelia, that Cordelia;
Yet they, should the last scene be there,
The great stage curtain about to drop,
If worthy their prominent part in the play,
Do not break up their lines to weep.
They know that Hamlet and Lear are gay;
Gaiety transfiguring all that dread.
All men have aimed at, found and lost;
Black out; Heaven blazing into the head:
Tragedy wrought to its uttermost.
Though Hamlet rambles and Lear rages,
And all the drop-scenes drop at once
Upon a hundred thousand stages,
It cannot grow by an inch or an ounce.

This assessment of Shakespeare's tragedies was written at the brink of Yeats's death and of the Second World War. Its way of assessing Shakespeare's achievement in these plays is to convert them into a static art form, symbolized by the images of three Chinamen carved on a piece of lapis lazuli:

There, on the mountain and the sky,
On all the tragic scene they stare.
One asks for mournful melodies;
Accomplished fingers begin to play.
Their eyes mid many wrinkles, their eyes,
Their ancient, glittering eyes, are gay.

My purpose is not to explicate Yeats's magnificent poem but to treat it as a piece of Shakespearean criticism. On the verge of death and world war Yeats could more easily turn to the tragedies of Shakespeare to support his poetic invention than confront directly the monumental problems of his time. For those tragedies do confront the problem of the continuance of civilization, or at least of the societies they are depicting, in ways that have been important for many centuries. I respond to Yeats's rhetoric and magic, but I wonder much about his easy disposal of those glittering eyes to look on a scene, which he immediately categorizes as tragic. If all of life is tragic, whether presented in lapis lazuli or in breath, then Shakespeare's tragedies had better be counted in. But this is not enough for Yeats, who must take the tragic and convert it into an overpowering interpretation of those tragedies that allows the actors to know even within the lines they speak and act and suffer, even within that limiting compass of art, "They know that Hamlet and Lear are gay; / Gaiety transfiguring all that dread." As a comment on Shakespeare, this is nonsense, and the nonsense begins with the total divorce between the moral issues of the plays and the effect we are asking them to make for us. The word "tragic" becomes merely the excuse, the all encompassing panacea, for not examining what it is that ails us or what happens in Shakespeare's tragedies. If everything is tragic and that tragedy is really gaiety, then we had better forget about trying to discern what is happening in these plays of Shakespeare.

It seems to me that this heresy of tragic gaiety, as Yeats would have us understand tragic knowledge, is nowhere more obvious than in the attempts of some of our most prominent critics to make the tragedy of Lear into a Christain experience. I see no way in which the suffering of Lear can be related to Christian redemption except in the way that Yeats transforms tragedy into gaiety, that is, by poetic fiat and not by examination of the text as delivered to us by Shakespeare in the early seventeenth century. The question has been argued intensely and is really two questions: Is *Lear* a Christian play? If the answer is no, then the second question emerges: Is Shakespeare a Christian writer? If the first question is answered affirmatively, then one must find a way in which the tragic knowledge of Lear leads him out of the trap he has set for himself, in which his love for Cordelia, poignantly revealed in act 4 and dexterously explicated by Professor McFarland, explains the ending of the play. If the question is answered negatively, then one is left with the further question of Shakespeare's adherence to the doctrines of Christianity as expounded in the sixteenth and seventeenth centuries. My own answer to these questions is no to the first and yes to the second. I think that Shakespeare is a profoundly Christian writer, and I think that *King Lear,* based as it is on historical sources, is meant to depict the plight of man before the Christian era, that is, before the salvation of man by Christ's sacrifice was available. The rest of this lecture will be devoted to proving this point, and my text, as announced in my title, will be "Nothing almost sees miracles."

We are so accustomed to making jokes about Nahum Tate's rewriting *Lear* with the happy ending of Edgar's marriage to Cordelia that we seldom take the time to observe that Tate was exercising not only his taste but also his historical sense, for all the historical sources from Geoffrey of Monmouth on inform us that Lear's and Cordelia's forces are victorious, that Lear reassumes the kingship and is succeeded by Cordelia, who rules the kingdom until she is defeated by her rebellious nephews, at which point she hangs herself in despair. The same story is told in the literary sources. *The True Chronicle Historie of King Leir and His Three Daughters Gonerill, Ragan, and Cordella* of 1605 in its final scene has the king of France announce the victory to Leir:

> KING. Thanks be to God, your foes are overcome,
> And you againe possessed of your right.
> LEIR. First to the heavens, next, thanks to you, my sonne,
> By whose good meanes I repossesse the same.[5]

The story is given by Spenser in the second book of *The Faerie Queene,* which continues the story beyond that given in *The True Chronicle Historie:*

> So to his crowne she him restor'd againe,
> In which he dyde, made ripe for death by eld,
> And after wild, it should to her remaine:
> Who peaceably the same long time did weld:
> And all mens harts in dew obedience held:
> Till that her sisters children, woxen strong

[5] *The True Chronicle Historie of King Leir and His Three Daughters Gonerill, Ragan, and Cordella,* in *Narrative and Dramatic Sources of Shakespeare,* ed. Geoffrey Bullough (London: Routledge & Kegan Paul, 1957-75), vol. 7, pp. 401-402.

Through proud ambition, against her rebeld,
And ouercommen kept in prison long,
Till wearie of that wretched life, her selfe she hong.
                                    (2.10.32)

The emphasis in all these accounts is on the restoration of
Lear. In all the sources, the story of Lear is cast in explicitly
Christian terms in which providential order is constantly in-
voked, even though the chroniclers make it very clear that the
story occurred about 800 B.C., at the same time as King Joash
of Israel.

Within the structure of mythical British history the story
of Lear plays a significant part. British history begins properly
with the triumph of Brute, the great-grandson of Aeneas, over
the giants, the aboriginal inhabitants of the island. The de-
scendants of Brute, that is, the Britains, rule until their extinct
line is replaced by the lawgiving rule of Mulmutius Donwallo,
whose dynasty extended until the invasion of Julius Caesar.
Lear is the tenth of the nineteen kings of the Britain period,
a period often mined by Elizabethan dramatists for their history plays. *Gorboduc*, the first English tragedy, is the story
of the eighteenth king, who ill-advisedly divides his kingdom
between his two sons Ferrex and Porrex. From this period
Shakespeare chose not only the story of Lear but also that of
Cymbeline, a king who reigned at the time of the Roman
invasion and is remembered only because he refused to pay
tribute money to Caesar and because his reign occurred just
before the birth of Christ. But more importantly, it is only in
the two plays based on this particular period of British history
that Shakespeare deviates significantly from his historical
sources. Granted his wholesale reliance on Holinshed for the
two tetralogies, why does he reverse the historical endings of
these two plays? In *Cymbeline* the king defeats the Romans,
which he does not do in the sources, and then turns around
and renders up the tribute money voluntarily, that is, he renders unto Caesar the things that are Caesar's. For the contin-
uation of that Biblical quotation and its significance for the

play, I refer you to the dissertation of my student Andrew Kelly.[6]

I can see no Biblical source to justify Shakespeare's changing the end of the Lear story, but it is Shakespeare and Shakespeare alone who creates the defeat of Lear. For the Jacobean audience brought up on the traditional history of Lear, Shakespeare's recasting of history must have been dramatically arresting. In the last scene of act 4 we see the moving reconciliation of Lear and Cordelia; on their exit Kent and a gentleman discuss the impending battle, and at the beginning of act 5 we listen to Goneril's and Regan's catlike solicitations of Edmund. The battle occurs as nothing more than a hiatus between two conversations between Edgar and Gloucester.

> EDGAR. Here, father, take the shadow of this tree
>   For your good host; pray that the right may thrive.
>   If ever I return to you again,
>   I'll bring you comfort.
> GLOUCESTER.   Grace go with you, sir.
>   *Exit* [EDGAR].
> *Alarum and retreat within.* [*Re*]*enter* EDGAR.
> EDGAR. Away, old man; give me thy hand; away!
>   King Lear hath lost, he and his daughter ta'en:
>   Give me thy hand; come on.
> GLOUCESTER. No further, sir; a man may rot even here.
> EDGAR. What, in ill thoughts again? Men must endure
>   Their going hence, even as their coming hither:
>   Ripeness is all. Come on.
> GLOUCESTER.   And that's true too.
>   (5.2.1-11)

In what must rank as the flattest line that Shakespeare ever wrote he disposes of Gloucester. The hopeful optimism of Edgar's first exit is matched by Gloucester's despair at the announcement of Lear's defeat. With this little scene Shakespeare has effectively severed himself from his historical

---

[6] Andrew Kelly, "*Cymbeline* Unravelled: A Study of Shakespeare's Allegory of Redemption" (Ph.D. dissertation, Princeton University, 1976).

sources and will now force the play to his intentions. With this scene the achieved reconciliation of Lear and Cordelia and the hoped-for victory in battle are dashed, and we immediately see the two new prisoners. Cordelia is still feisty: "Shall we not see these daughters and these sisters?" Lear, content to bask in the love of his daughter, delivers two of the most moving speeches that Shakespeare ever wrote. The first one, "No, no, no, no! Come, let's away to prison," despite its emotional appeal, is a total capitulation to the defeat that Shakespeare is insisting on, and it is affirmed by Edmund's brusque "Take them away." Lear's second speech, "Upon such sacrifices, my Cordelia, / The gods themselves throw incense," shows the turbulence within the man and his unspecified hatred against those who have led him to acquiesce to his golden imprisonment:

> He that parts us shall bring a brand from heaven,
> And fire us hence like foxes. Wipe thine eyes;
> The good years shall devour them, flesh and fell,
> Ere they shall make us weep. We'll see 'em starv'd first.
> Come.
>
> (5.3.22-26)[7]

Nothing of this will happen except the weeping. The submerged violence of Lear's response, his total rejection of any of the causes that have brought him to this pass, his refusal to recognize the pertinence of Cordelia's assessment of the situation as a problem of "these daughters and these sisters," and his hatred of those forces he is still unwilling even to name do not make this scene the lyric interlude that most critical readings try to make it; Shakespeare sees to that. Between the exit of Lear and Cordelia and our next thought of them the major evil forces of the play are disposed of: the daughters and sisters have disposed of themselves and Edmund is in his dying gasps, when enter Kent:

---

[7] For the various Biblical echoes in this passage see Thomas Carter, *Shakespeare and Holy Scripture* (London: Hodder and Stoughton, 1905), p. 442.

> I am come
> To bid my king and master aye good night:
> Is he not here?
> ALBANY.   Great thing of us forgot!
>   (5.3.236-238)

Indeed, Albany's inability to manage the life of the stage in-
dicts the entire audience, for we too have forgotten Lear and
Cordelia in our restless attempt to give to the evil characters
what we have been aching to do throughout the play. We are
so much in the habit of excusing Lear's division of the kingdom as an adjunct of "the fairy tale," Cordelia as Cinderella,
the other two sisters playing their assigned roles, and Lear as
wicked stepmother, that we do not see that this mythic imposition really does not help our understanding of the play
so long as we hold on to wicked stepmother as our hero, good
old King Lear. Certainly the fairy tale aspect of the beginning
has shrunk to meaninglessness by the time of Lear's and Cordelia's reconciliation at the end of the fourth act. What I
would like to suggest is that the last act of the play is equally
a nightmare fairy tale released from the pressures of time when
Shakespeare departs from his historical sources—when Edgar
announces the defeat of Lear and his daughter. From this
point on Shakespeare hammers home to us his relentless and
hopeless intention.

Shakespeare does not show us the decisive battle between
the forces of Lear and his renegade daughters. We are shown
instead the ascendancy of Edmund, the bastard, as the master
of the show. Cornwall is dead, leaving Regan free; Goneril
is still encumbered by the weak Albany, who is now the rank-
ing official of the kingdom, but it is clearly Edmund in control,
in control of so much that the center will not hold. The battle
we have not seen is shifted to a chivalric combat between
Edmund the bastard and his disguised brother, legitimate Edgar. Regan, poisoned, leaves before the combat. Goneril, in
despair at the wounding of Edmund, runs off to kill herself,
and Edmund, slowly divesting himself of evil and of life, re-
counts little by little the ways in which he has controlled the

153

situation; he and his brother are reconciled, and the story of Gloucester's death is told (which, if I am not mistaken, should be one of the sources for Yeats's tragic joy). Kent enters and asks the question that reminds us of that "great thing of us forgot"; the bodies of the dead sisters are brought onto the stage, and Edmund remarks

> Yet Edmund was beloved:
> The one the other poisoned for my sake,
> And after slew herself.
> ALBANY. Even so. Cover their faces.
> EDMUND. I pant for life: some good I mean to do,
> Despite of mine own nature. Quickly send,
> Be brief in it, to th' castle; for my writ
> Is on the life of Lear and on Cordelia:
> Nay, send in time.
>
> (5.3.241-249)

Edmund's comments are exactly the kind of moral reversal we await in a soap opera, or in Verdi, the ineluctable espousal of the good at the final moment. But that is not, I think, how Shakespeare saw these penultimate lines of Edmund. Why does he not leave Edmund to be the bastard he has been throughout the play? I do not want to gainsay Edmund's desire to "do" some good, but I think that we cannot read this passage merely as disposal of the villain. More is at stake than a sentimental reversal of "personality" traits and received traditions. The disposition of Edmund's evil requires more than a moral response. The issues in this play are not merely whether one is good or bad, not even whether or not one repents from evil ways, although Edmund apparently does after his fight with Edgar (5.3.162ff). It is Edgar, the apparently ineffectual true son, he who has mortally wounded his bastard brother in righteous combat, who wants to exchange charity. But in what seems to be a reversal of Edmund's bastardy, to Edgar's plea for an exchange of charity, that ultimate renunciation of vengeance, that ultimate turning of the other cheek, Edmund responds with total misapprehension: "Yet Edmund was beloved." His consolation is the illicit love of Lear's two married daughters, and his proof of their love for him is that one poisoned the other and then slew herself. This is indeed true, as the play tells us, but it seems an inauspicious augur of reconciliation. But the weakness of the forces of good is only too apparent:

> ALBANY. Run, run, O, run!
> EDGAR. To who, my lord? Who has the office? Send
> Thy token of reprieve.

Edgar's questions are necessarily addressed to Albany, but they are answered by Edmund:

> Well thought on: take my sword,
> Give it the captain
> EDGAR.   Haste thee for thy life.

and then Edmund's final speech addressed to Albany:

> He hath commission from thy wife and me
> To hang Cordelia in the prison, and
> To lay the blame upon her own despair,
> That she fordid herself.
> ALBANY. The gods defend her! Bear him hence awhile.
> (5.3.249-258)

The astonishing thing about this bit of stagecraft is that Edmund in his death throes is still in control. It is he and the dead daughters who have imposed the true historical death of Cordelia on the character in the play. The evil of Edmund overrides the happy ending of Lear in history and brings Cordelia's despairing ending into the fiction of the play. Like the battle, which in history Lear and Cordelia won, their happy reigns become simply a hiatus in the triumph of evil.

But Shakespeare is still managing his play. The still-living evil Edmund is borne off at the behest of Albany, leaving the two dead bodies of the evil sisters, and, as Bradley pointed out many years ago, with Albany's cry, "The gods defend her," the answer given is "*Enter* LEAR, *with* CORDELIA *in his arms.*" For Bradley as for many later critics, this ironic entrance raises doubts about Shakespeare's belief in the gods. I disagree with that assessment completely; I think the entrance calls our assessment of Lear into question. For from this point on he and his three dead daughters are alone on stage, with the sole support of Albany, Edgar, and Kent as chorus. All active evil has been stopped; there are no more threats to Lear or to the sovereignty of his kingdom, and the ancient Lear takes center stage. Shakespeare, in releasing him from the happiness of the historical sources, places full responsibility on him for the ending of the play.

What tragic knowledge does Lear bring to this artistic responsibility? Great dramatic force. Poignancy. The willing approval of his followers, none of whom is capable of dealing with the problem of this old man or of his kingdom. That they love him helps no more than that Cordelia loved him. It did not work, and it did not work because Shakespeare did not want it to work. He wanted Lear to be a failure, poignant, but a failure, certainly no hero, or Shakespeare need not have rewritten history.

One of the most interesting Christian interpretations of the play, one that I espoused for a number of years, claims a kind of transcendence for Lear based on the double plot. Even as we see Gloucester being guided by Edgar from misapprehension, to rejection of his blind despair, through rejection of his senses, to the unacknowledged comfort in his death, so Lear is led by an invisible actor who will lead us all beyond the misery of the play and our lives. But I can no longer believe in the saving grace of double plots.[8] The ending of *Lear* is as bleak and unrewarding as man can reach outside the gates of hell. There is no transcendence that we ourselves do not impose on the play. Every gesture of Lear's love is countered by an equal and opposite gesture of hatred. "Thou must be patient" is countered by "Howl, howl, howl, howl!" Every optimistic surmise by any character who calls upon the gods is denied.

Things fall apart; the centre cannot hold;

[8] See Sherman Hawkins, "The Kingdom and Trials of Love—Theology in *King Lear*," *University: A Princeton Magazine*, no. 19 (Winter 1963-64), pp. 3-9.

Mere anarchy is loosed upon the world,
The blood-dimmed tide is loosed, and everywhere
The ceremony of innocence is drowned;
The best lack all conviction, while the worst
Are full of passionate intensity.
Surely some revelation is at hand;
Surely the Second Coming is at hand.

I do not choose these portentously prophetic lines from Yeats's "Second Coming" idly. The despairing description of the state of the world can be equally applied to Lear, and the revelation, that Second Coming Yeats was prophesying, can be equally applied to the time Shakespeare knew could only be before the advent of Christ. The changes Shakespeare made in history to give shape to his play, to the unknowing figure of his king, owe much to his perception that Lear lived in a time when there was no salvation, no revelation, no help for humanity in its fallen condition. "Nothing will come of nothing." The reconciliation of Lear and Cordelia cannot prosper in an un-saved world. Lear divides his kingdom and hopes for the best from fallen man; he is deceived, and in death he is deluded by something he cannot hope for.

Throughout the play Lear has asked for more than he can possibly get. He asks more from Cordelia than she can say and illogically deprives himself of kingdom and of love. When he sees his man Kent in the stocks, he cries, "Who put my man in the stocks?" But he lacks the power and the insight to remedy the situation except through the impotent "O reason not the need." In his madness on the heath he levels all human responsibility to "None does offend, none I say." His defeat in battle he counters with "no, no, no, no! Come, let's away to prison." On bearing in the dead body of Cordelia, he can blame only the men of stone, who are in reality the only sustaining forces he has known throughout the play. Lear still cannot tell good from evil, or to put it more kindly, true from false, and we find ourselves in a more battered version of the ignorance he displayed at the beginning of the play. Lear finally sees nothing. He has passed beyond the sympathy of Edgar, Kent, and Albany. The resolution of the play offers no hope, and this irresolution is imaged in two speeches in the last scene of the play.

The first is the three half-line responses of Kent, Edgar, and Albany to Lear's entry, "Howl, howl, howl, howl!"

> I know when one is dead and when one lives;
> She's dead as earth. Lend me a looking-glass;
> If that her breath will mist or stain the stone,
> Why, then she lives.
> KENT.   Is this the promised end?
> EDGAR. Or image of that horror?
> ALBANY.   Fall and cease.

Two questions have been asked after that shattering and impossible affirmation made by the old king. They are spoken by the two most faithful supporters of the Lear and Gloucester plots, and their litanylike half lines present a genuine problem of interpretation. I agree with most editors that they refer to the Last Judgment, but we should not be too quick to bring in that devastating and total finality at this point in this play without understanding how the reference applies to the situation. I assume that Kent's "Is this the promised end?" grows out of his incredulous observation of Lear and the dead Cordelia. In and of itself the phrase need not refer to the Last Judgment, but can mean merely "Is this what we can look forward to at the end?" It is only with Edgar's half line that the allusion becomes a certainty, because that half line is a reading of and a response to Kent's words.

It should also be observed that each half line takes up a diametrically opposed vision of the Last Judgment, the first emphasizing the promise, the second the horror; both together constitute the whole image of that day of conflagration. Kenneth Muir, in his notes to the Arden edition, refers the reader to two provocative earlier statements in the play that lead us beyond the immediate dramatic ambiance. The first is Gloucester asking to kiss the hand of Lear.

LEAR. Let me wipe it first; it smells of mortality.

GLOUCESTER. O ruined piece of Nature! This great world
   Shall so wear out to nought.

(4.6.133-135)

Lear displays an uncanny vulnerability in emphasizing his
mortality, and Gloucester generalizes on a fallen (ruined) nature betraying itself to nought (with a pun on naughtiness).
Muir relates this line to a passage in act 3, scene 1, when
Kent's concern over the whereabouts of the king is answered
by a gentleman:

> Contending with the fretful elements;
> Bids the wind blow the earth into the sea,
> Or swell the curlèd waters 'bove the main,
> That things might change or cease; tears his white hair,
> Which the impetuous blasts, with eyeless rage,
> Catch in their fury, and make *nothing* of.

(3.1.4-9)

What interests me in Muir's suggested comparisons is the
assessment of Lear's regal presumption against his mortality
and the nature against which he is raging. Both lead the reader
back to that *topos* of nothingness that has unremittingly
beaten against the forces of love throughout this play. It is
the nothing that Cordelia speaks at the beginning and the end
of the play. I suppose that no audience has ever taken that
nothingness as anything less than all, and we are all assured
of this at the beginning of the play. But the question I have
been asking throughout this essay is whether Lear sees at the
end that nothing is all. The question is complicated because
our decision whether nothing is all or nothing depends on our
view of the world, which leads me back to those two half
lines of Kent and Edgar. Is this the promised end or image of
that horror? No answer is given in the play to either of these
questions, except Albany's even more enigmatic "Fall and
cease." One wonders to whom this speech is addressed, for
many have already fallen, already ceased.

    This is surely not a simple Christian resolution as Professor
Seltzer shows, but it raises all the problems of authorial intent

and audience response, and that intent and response were, I suggest strongly, toward a providential view of history, toward a hierarchical view of society, toward a moral view of human action. In my view Shakespeare is not showing us the meaninglessness of history, nor the tyranny of society, nor the psychological needs of fathers, daughters, or bastards, nor even the limitation and duplicity of language, except as contained within a providential, hierarchical, moral, and linguistic world in which the central figure of this play fails to understand the language ("Nothing will come of nothing. Speak again") and the morality ("I am a man / More sinned against than sinning") and the hierarchy ("our darker purpose . . . while we / Unburthened crawl toward death") and that Providence in which so few of us any longer believe that we hardly think that Shakespeare might have included Lear in it. I think he did. For Shakespeare the story of Lear was part of history, and all of history was part of that providential plan that would eventually bring good out of evil. But Shakespeare changes Lear's success in history to defeat in fiction. Many may think that this Shakespearean invention of Lear's defeat is Shakespeare's growth beyond the Providence, hierarchy, and morality that I advocate as the proper context in which to read Shakespeare's play, but I think that the man who later invented Leontes and Prospero had not grown beyond the thinking of his time because the resolution of their sorrows need not be separated from the orthodox Christian view of life. Leontes repents, because of which Shakespeare, with a free and loving hand, gives him back his child and wife, a generosity more than his source will allow. Prospero, with almost providential power, learns to behave humanly, not to revenge, not to punish, but to love and finally to abjure his magical powers by which he accomplished the resolution both for his enemies and more importantly for himself.

The major tragedies of Shakespeare seem to be uncomfortable within the frame of what we call the Elizabethan world picture only because we have set up another frame for what we take to be tragedy. We lament the impossibility of tragedy in the modern world because we have romanticized our own heroic inadequacies, understanding neither heroism nor inadequacy. What Shakespeare saw as all too human failure we have converted into triumph, unjustified and undefined. What separates the Willie Lomans from the Lears and Hamlets is, not nobility, not even literary skill, but an honest look at what we are demanding of Shakespeare, which is just another way of saying what we are imposing on him. I am deeply moved by the last scene of *Lear*; the image of the old man bent over the dead body of his one loving daughter is appalling, but it does not obscure the fact that two other daughters are also dead on stage and three men stand nearby, one of whom was husband to one of those unloved and unnoticed bodies. It does not matter that we know morally that those other two merit no attention. They are there in spite of Lear's too late devotion to Cordelia. Their presence on stage is essential in production, for we are again back to the opening of the play in which all three spoke nothing. What has Lear learned? Nothing. Not even suffering has taught him anything. His attention in this last scene is too late given to the one daughter, but it might equally be said that attention of another sort might be given to the other two. Nothing.

The final speech, whether it should be spoken by Albany or by Edgar, is four of the strangest lines ever written by Shakespeare:

> The weight of this sad time we must obey,
> Speak what we feel, not what we ought to say.
> The oldest hath borne most: we that are young
> Shall never see so much, nor live so long.

What is the weight of time? And how do we obey it? One can only suppose that the weight of this sad time is the death of Lear and the failure of the "gor'd state." The main problem is whether the lines are merely descriptive or evaluations of the situation. The speech verges on plangent tautology: it does not take into account all the currents of the play unless we assign each particular cadence to a figure in the drama. Speak what we feel (Cordelia), not what we ought to say (Regan and Goneril); the oldest hath borne most (Lear): we that are young (Albany, Kent, Edgar) shall never see so much, nor live so long.[9] How are we to assess the truth of these statements? Cordelia did speak what she felt, but the second half of that line, "not what we ought to say," is an indictment, not of the two other sisters, but of the world in which Cordelia's truth is bound to be taken as a lie. The "oldest hath borne most" can only refer to Lear ("I am a man / More sinned against than sinning"). But between that cadence and the final one, we must acknowledge that Lear's bearing before and throughout the play has produced the death of his daughters and of a good many others. The resolution of the speech "we that are young / Shall never see so much, nor live so long" is a question that we must abide because we cannot verify it. That they will not live so long is simple conjecture, that they will not see so much depends entirely on what it is we see. I would like to suggest that, with the vision of three dead daughters and one dead king, the weight we must obey is total failure in fact and in vision. "Nothing *almost* sees miracles but misery."

[9] I am sure that I owe this division of this last speech to a lecture by Maynard Mack, which I heard as an undergraduate.

Eight

King Lear
in the Theater

Daniel Seltzer

These lectures have been seven rough acts to follow, not only for their learning, for which I owe them much, inevitably altering my own anticipated approaches as I sat listening and admiring, but because here and there have been points of disagreement—and, perhaps, if I can state my disagreements in the right ways, I can work toward some new approaches that help illuminate other facets of Shakespeare's talent in the theater. If I fail, I shall at least have supported the view of my old teacher, the late Alfred Harbage, who ended his British Academy lecture by observing that after all Shakespeare is inexhaustible, though his commentators are not.

My title, "*King Lear* in the Theater," does not mean that I will talk about famous or infamous productions of the past, though I cannot overlook certain aspects of theater history, such as the fact that Shakespeare alone of all those who told and retold the Lear story, as Professor Roche has cogently observed, changed the major details of its ending, and that they remained changed, through Cibber and Garrick and Kean until Dickens's great friend, Macready, restored the original in the middle of the nineteenth century. Nor does my title imply an apologia for the very theatricality of the play; in other words, I do not take up the argument against the Romantic critics who claimed that this is a great poem but not a great play. Surely we all know by now that that is not correct, but we also know why they, even the most perceptive of them, may have been led to think they were right, given the productions they saw. I want rather to speak of something harder to pin down, harder to explain, for there is a minimal critical vocabulary, at least in common academic usage, to describe the phenomenon I wish to describe. I want to speak of the experience of *King Lear* in the theater, which means, not only Lear's experience but also how this can affect ours—while acknowledging, of course, that each member of an audience will inevitably bring different habits of perception to the play. I suggest that, as different as these habits may be, any significant production of *Lear* will eventually cause them to bear a general likeness, not because, or primarily because, a great play evokes a strange and even occult similarity among the sensations and thoughts it elicits among the many who see, hear, and feel it, but because it is a provable fact of theatrical life that great stage works have an implicit architecture, an organic shape, which traces, almost as though one could project this shape pictorially as well as aurally, gently yet firmly a set of limits that the play will bear—or, to put it another way, an aural and visual architecture that within itself will allow great variety, but that simultaneously offers up a specificity of emotion and meaning that are indeed finite and that to change will cause the play, in the jargon of the profession, to fail "to read," to fail to make human sense. Indeed, some of the most interesting stretches of time on the Shakespearean stage are when Shakespeare himself breaks the rules of the harmonies he has already set for himself, or introduces a dissonance of characterization or event that causes the whole drama to wobble dangerously. The grit, rigor, and depth of Angelo and Isabella, woven conspicuously into *Measure for Measure*, are examples of what I mean in theatrical terms; so indeed is Shylock himself, who clearly weighs so much emotionally that his ballast almost, but not quite, causes *The Merchant of Venice* to founder. The discomfort we may feel as the drama moves forward in time is related to an interpretation of the text that, in spite of its great potential for variety, has still a built-in emotional logic, which even very different kinds of audience members will feel. This sensation, when the boundaries of the play itself are maintained in production, is very much like the aesthetic relief we know and feel when a symphony of the classical period returns finally either to its basic key or one musically related to it.

The experience of *King Lear* in the theater is simultaneously King Lear's experience of himself in the theater and our conscious or subconscious perception of that experience. Part of my lecture will try to explain this. A discussion of this double experience—his of his own and ours of his—is related to the theatrical process we call tragedy. I am not intellectually equipped, nor would it be appropriate here, to discuss all of this immense process, but it might help if one observes a few things it is not, or at least a few things that Elizabethan and Jacobean tragedies are not. In the remarkably short number of years that separate, say, the middle or late 1580s and the astounding achievement of Shakespeare, even in his early years, not to mention the period of his deepest probings of the human condition, serious stage works (romances as well as plays called tragedies) became mainly secularized. Many retained clear vestiges of religious signals and general ambiance in their words and deeds. Shylock himself, as Professor Danson has discussed in his most recent book, is such a vestige, or a large part of him is, and, without doing damage to the play, perhaps must be so understood. The same is true of Iago. But however often the texture of the play may contain a dramaturgical allusiveness to the Old and the New Laws, for example, the theatrical experience of the whole drama is not, as one might say, about them. When Othello clasps Desdemona's face between his hands and predicts "ill-starred wench! / Pale as thy smock! When we shall meet at compt, / This look of thine will hurl my soul from heaven, / And fiends will snatch at it," he is anticipating damnation for himself. But whether or not he is to be damned when the rest becomes silence is not what concerned Shakespeare at this juncture. Faustus is damned, and his vivid descent, plummeting through a trapdoor, is indeed a real event in the last moments of Marlowe's plot. Experientially, in the theater, what is involving Marlowe, Faustus, and us, too, is the human makeup of that sort of man who knows what he must do to be saved and can no more do it than Coriolanus can apologize to the curs of Rome.

My good friend Professor Roche quoted a number of final speeches during his excellent lecture, and, if I understood him correctly, these quotations were set forth, not to prove that the plays in any simple sense "taught a lesson," but that at least they were conceived as artifice based on a mode of thinking didactic and philosophical in the broadest sense—a mode that would require playwright, performer, and spectator to understand a moral idea, usually one relating to the Christian universe in which the dramas were composed. I think that to approach Shakespeare's plays in this way is at best dangerous and can be misleading, simply because it is not in the nature of the greatest drama written after the middle 1580s to teach, or to do that only. Nor am I swerving from my subject as widely as it may seem. A character's experience of himself, and therefore ours of him or her, does relate to tragic effect; and this effect, or effectiveness in theatrical performance, whatever it meant for the Greeks (though Aristotle can be highly suggestive in this regard), did not for Shakespeare's audiences mean a lesson of any sort, or at least not a lesson necessarily related to the major emotional power of the plays. By the time Shakespeare was writing (roughly two plays a year, and doing very well at it), Elizabethan drama had become (as any historical scholar will be the first to tell us) perhaps the most impure, the most mixed mode of writing yet experienced. It was a combination of more genres, more species and subspecies of literary—and sometimes hardly literary— endeavor than any other writing between the late medieval drama (which was very attractively and, at its best, perhaps successfully and purely didactic) and the works of Samuel Beckett (whose comment on his first and latest biography, as he might put it, suggests strongly that he could not care less about "lessons").

Drama is a phenomenon of human experience, which, for its creator, its performer, and its spectator, conjures up not an imitative mirror or vision of life, no matter how Hamlet puts it, but, because of the nature of the experience, real life itself. This may seem heretical, for we have all been warned for years, as we dragged our weary paths through colleges and graduate schools, that the people of drama are not "real" people; they are fictional creations, and primarily literary ones at that. But I am suggesting that what may be true in *A Passage to India* or *Tom Jones*, or in *The Waste Land* and innumerable and great poems by Stevens and Frost, is not true of drama at its best, and when performed best. What I am trying to express may relate, if he will allow me to say so, to some of Professor Goldman's remarks about the verbal—and therefore the emotional—specificity of drama. The whole effect in the theater of that little button that Lear wants undone, or of the vile jelly within poor Gloucester's eye sockets, is most effective—that is, most theatrically telling—when we are convinced, even against our wills, that these are specific and real objects, and that the characters' reactions to them are not holding any mirror up to life as though life were offstage in a wing, but are precisely creating new life before us, at that very moment, in this very place, on the stage itself. Shakespearean characters become real people, and Shakespeare may have been the first dramatist in western tradition to discover how to make them so. Therefore, the endings of their lives, which we call tragic, are sometimes as mixed, even as contradictory, as human, as their experience, and ours, of their lives in preceding hours. Lear has just as great a tendency for self-pity, not an admirable trait, at the moment before he expires as he had earlier. Macbeth goes out fighting: it is a natural reflex after a moment of superstitious fear. And any of us who have known not simply infatuation but the all-consuming, joyfully diseased possessiveness and needs of insecure love knows what Othello implies when he admits that he has loved not wisely but too well, and then chooses to tell an anecdote, which, for him, encapsulates those better parts that have been corrupted.

I do not know what "tragic knowledge" means either, and I suspect, as does Professor Roche, that it is a misleading phrase. But for me the most suggestive observation Aristotle made about those Greek tragedies he chose to discuss was his all too short reference to what he called *anagnorisis*, which may be best translated as "in-sight." I would like to emphasize the sound of that hyphen between the two words: it draws our attention to that power which sees innerly, whereas the ability to do so was lacking before. "Lay on, Macduff; / And damned be him that first cries, 'Hold, enough' " is only the literal point at which Macbeth's stage life disappears; surely this hero, who has the most capacious imagination of them all, sees inwardly with most theatrical power about eight minutes earlier in the play. I am still wending my way toward *Lear*, I assure you, but you must first hear once again what must be the most often memorized soliloquy in the canon, but possibly also the best one in all the plays, more suggestive, more honest, less complaining, and more "in-sightful" even than that other most famous one, that long, brilliant exposition on suicide by a very bright, analytical, and somewhat superannuated graduate student:

> She should have died hereafter;
> There would have been a time for such a word.
> Tomorrow, and tomorrow, and tomorrow
> Creeps in this petty pace from day to day,
> To the last syllable of recorded time;
> And all our yesterdays have lighted fools
> The way to dusty death. Out, out, brief candle!
> Life's but a walking shadow, a poor player
> That struts and frets his hour upon the stage
> And then is heard no more. It is a tale
> Told by an idiot, full of sound and fury,
> Signifying nothing.
>
> (*Macbeth*, 5.5.17-28)

It is not my business, nor would it be appropriate here, to explore this aria to its depths, even were I capable of it. But it may be worth observing that little more than a decade and a half before that speech was composed (before its experience in the theater) many corresponding characters in Tudor interludes, their didactic and, at that time, theatrical point being the dangers of despair, would have lamented their state in jogging fourteeners, and then witnessed to their horror the entrance of the Vice figure, the emissary of Satan himself, bearing a noose, and announcing in glee that just outside is a tree, which, with the help of this rope, will end all the hero's misery. Several hundred plays written before *Macbeth* and after 1500 are extant, and, for a reason that has nothing to do with our concerns here, I once read them all. About twenty-five contain didactic episodes more or less as I have described; the dialogues are often interchangeable, for those jigging veins of rhyming mother wits had not yet discovered what Shakespeare soon learned: that the recreation of human feelings in the theater will not bear the weight of pure dogma; that feelings, projected with the aid of the specificity of language, will actually effect new life on stage, given those almost occult talents of a good actor (another subject which Professor Goldman has discussed with great range and wit); and that finally, and perhaps most important, the recreation of a human life through language, movement, objects, and space will automatically, whether willed or not by a good playwright, a good actor, and a good audience, cause to exist a viable psychological life below or, if you like, beyond the level of words and movements themselves. I am aware that this should be a scholarly paper, and that I have just paraphrased what people in the theater call a subtext, but a little Stanislavski will do none of us any harm. That Macbeth is in a dangerous state of despair is undeniable, but that is obviously not what either his life or the play has been about. Another great religiously derived command hovers through the thick darkness, gore, and rooky woods of this play: the commandment says, "Thou shalt not kill." But I hope we can agree that, although the play *Macbeth* incorporates the resonance of this commandment in its total action, it is not the purpose of the drama to teach us not to kill.

I said that Shakespeare's art was incredibly mixed; one might even say, without pejorative connotation, that his dramaturgy was the most impure of all playwrights'. Romeo dashes, in the understandable haste of passion, toward the door of the Friar's cell, and Lawrence's warning—in this case—is a much greater part of the meaning, if I may use that word, of the play: "They stumble that run fast." Certainly more than the awful stumblings of the two leading characters takes place; for one thing, Juliet first and later Romeo become better poets. But they do not discover in themselves, and therefore cannot project to us, that huge ambiguity which, in Shakespearean tragedy, only comes after one has known himself but slenderly, an inwardly directed and hard to articulate acceptance of human responsibility. That reason must rule the passions, just as God rules mankind, was a medieval and an Elizabethan commonplace; and indeed perhaps one of the reasons why *Romeo and Juliet* resonates more of simple errors, if it be not a comedy of them, than of deep human discovery is precisely that its emotional limits do not exceed, or not very far anyway, how it hurts to stumble when you run too fast. But one could hardly say that *Antony and Cleopatra*, for example, derives its major emotional energy from showing what will happen to a general who follows a queen whose warships' sails are clotted with sparrows' nests (emblems of lust). All of these characters do of course exhibit more than a common share of real, honest-to-goodness concupiscence; and of course it carries with it, as it does today or any day, great danger and results, in these plays, in vast destruction. But I am trying to say that, in theatrical terms, the great plays—and not only Shakespeare's in this period—are not primarily concerned with that, or with dramatic evocation of any primarily moral question. For example, though your teachers and mine have made much through the years of the great danger King Lear invites when he divides his kingdom (and no doubt *Gorboduc* and other examples articulate this belief commonly held in the period), in no line of *King Lear* is this particular piece of Lear's foolishness mentioned even once. Shakespeare verbalizes potential dangers more powerfully than any other dramatist when he considers them necessary for development of his action, and he elaborates with excruciating surgery Lear's other wrongdoings, with nothing stinted. For he allows, and I suspect wants, the old man to curse his way through the first half of the play with all his own inhumane acts on his head.

Let me summarize what I have tried to say so far, and then deal more specifically with *King Lear* itself.

First, it is well to think of the experience of this play, or any other of true significance, as an experience that exists among playwright, character, and audience simultaneously, for drama is a social art and demands mutuality of action and reaction, stimulus and response.

Second, because this is so, great dramas, while they will almost certainly deal with philosophical and moral issues and actions, rely more on evocation of feeling than upon ideas, didactic or not, which lend themselves to our familiar modes of literary or historical analysis or both. In fact, the phenomena of performance resist these modes.

Third, because such plays are full of characters who are striving to speak what they feel, or striving to hide what they feel, or plainly are ignorant of what they really want to feel or cannot yet feel, great dramatic personalities always project, with their spoken words, a subtextual script that works contrapuntally with the written one, the whole orchestration creating a structure of emotions just as surely as sequences of episodic events, speeches, and the length of these events and speeches create that with which we are more familiar—a literary structure.

Fourth, because the actor must actually create a closed circuit between feelings felt and words spoken—in other words, because in the greatest drama there must always be reasons for actions and speech—a life is energized on stage that is purely real and not imitative. For this reason, the final effect of the stage process we call tragedy is an effect that necessarily enlarges one's emotional stamina and rigor of imagination more than it relies on brain power, the character's or ours: at the end of great tragedy "reason [is] in itself confounded." To "speak what we feel, not what we ought to say" means (whatever else it means) that language is not as powerful as emotion, and that the best use of language at times such as these is to serve emotion as best it can.

The shape of any play in performance is visual, aural, and temporal. It maintains the condition of music and adds images

of action actually seen and experienced. We need a new vocabulary to describe these phenomena, though the text itself
will never cease to be of first importance, for it will remain
our primary source of other data. These data are three in
number—forces felt and understood by the actors and, to the
extent that the actors have inhabited them, by an audience.
Everything and anything that happens on stage (in any play)
belongs to one of these three bodies of data, which are built
incrementally through stage time, much as sounds accumulate
during a musical performance both at the present moment of
their sounding and in the memory of the audience. This me-
morial recall is as important for character and spectator as
it is for a baroque composer, Bach, for example, in his solo
violin or cello suites and partitas, who counts on our retention
of a single note while a harmony is formed of that remembered
sound and a new one. These three components of performed
drama are, first, *rhythm*, having to do with the tempo and
pace of physical and verbal activity in time; second, *images*,
having to do both with a continuity of words or clusters of
similar words and—what we usually forget—the images of
what is seen: bodies, light or its absence, objects, and the like;
and, third, the projection of *ideas*, which means exactly what
it says if we recall the caveat that no great play is ever about
ideas (or only about them), though all characters, even stupid
ones, have them and often articulate them.

The continuities of these elements of acting determine a
performance's shape (I realize I am mixing metaphors and
welcome suggestions for greater clarification). Perhaps one
should say simply that these dramatic elements bring about
a sequence of energies or intensities, each relating to the actor's
projection in words and actions of both his inner and physical
life. But a slow rhythm, for example, need not by any means
effect low energy; for example:

> Now, our joy,
> Although our last and least; to whose young love
> The vines of France and milk of Burgundy
> Strive to be interest; what can you say to draw

A third more opulent than your sisters? Speak.
CORDELIA. Nothing, my lord.
LEAR. Nothing?
CORDELIA. Nothing.
LEAR. Nothing will come of nothing. Speak again.

(1.1.82-90)

Although the rhythm is slow, the energy here is no lower than it is in cursing, that form of speech which seems most congenial to this harsh, peremptory old man in almost the whole first third of the play:

Let it be so, thy truth then be thy dower!
For, by the sacred radiance of the sun,
The mysteries of Hecate and the night,
By all the operation of the orbs
From whom we do exist and cease to be,
Here I disclaim all my paternal care,
Propinquity and property of blood,
And as a stranger to my heart and me
Hold thee from this for ever. The barbarous Scythian,
Or he that makes his generation messes
To gorge his appetite, shall to my bosom
Be as well neighbored, pitied, and relieved,
As thou my sometime daughter.

(1.1.108-120)

I have spoken several times of the shape of a play. This aural and active graph of action is much more than simple plot, though narrative sequence underpins it. The shape of a play is determined by the sequential intensities of inner and expressed feelings; and these determine, or are determined by, subtle sequences of rhythms, images, and ideas. The shape to which I am referring has very little to do with act and scene divisions. I think it will illumine the theatrical experience of a Shakespeare play to describe its sequence of greater and lesser intensities in terms of movements, borrowing the symphonic word. Similarly, rhythmic units within movements might be called phrases of action, and (here borrowing, not from Stanislavski, but from his students and followers) the smallest unit or process of action within a phrase might be termed a beat.

In theatrical jargon "beat" is a useful word, for it reminds us in still another way that a play approaches the condition of music, that it exists inevitably in flux, and never quite the same way twice. I have elsewhere defined a beat so as to remind us always of this passage of time, and have told my own students that they should think of it as that passage of stage time between the initiation of an intention or need within a character and either its completion or deflection. For example, the beat that begins when Lear turns to Cordelia, needing desperately for her to offer even greater praise to win more land, and ends with "Let it be so, thy truth then be thy dower!" is a deflected beat. In a director's notebook, *Lear* would doubtless be scored in several thousand beats. But I think that *Lear* is also a paradigm for almost all of Shakespearean drama in that it consists of three large movements (and not five acts). The first movement ends with Lear's expulsion to the heath; the second consists of what we call the storm scenes, and ends with the Fool's cryptic good night at noon; the third begins with Gloucester's blinding (act 3, scene 7) and continues through the end of the offstage battle and Lear's little hymn to Cordelia on the way to prison; and finally (I may be begging the question here), as in other long works with a dense contrapuntal texture, there is a quick and highly intense coda, from the duel to the last words of the play.

The characters with whom the play is most concerned will live their lives on stage not only within this aural and visual architecture but also in a certain sequence of exposures—exposures to us of their experience. Though I admit the device is an artificial one, and useful only to clarify the leading character's passage through his stage life, let us sketch out as succinctly as possible the sequence of Lear's exposures to us. We are so used to thinking automatically of the complexities of these big plays, I think you will be surprised to learn that Lear himself holds the stage—that is, demands specificity of focus because of his spoken or physical action—only eleven times in the entire play. (For that matter, it never ceases to surprise me that in *Hamlet*—a play that Shakespeare surely must have elaborated and for which he must have allowed himself certain additional material, which would have been at least partially cut in performance—in that gigantic convoluted theatrical discourse, the title role holds the focus in only fifteen beats of stage activity.)

The first movement of *Lear* (citing only those beats that purely concern Lear himself) shows us the division of the kingdom; the scene in which he returns from the hunt, meets Kent, is insulted by Oswald, is riddled by the Fool, and curses Goneril; the little scene with the Fool, as they wait for horses; and the huge phrase of action that begins with Kent in the stocks, and goes on through Lear's arrival, Regan's and Goneril's carving away the number of his knights, ending with his great expostulation on human need. Throughout, the energy is high, the rhythms harsh and syncopated, and the visual and verbal images kaleidoscopic and elaborate—that is, they are so except for one scene, of which I wish to remind you. This scene illustrates the character's temperament not only as we have seen it but also as it has begun to modulate, as his imagination moves to spaces more generous than his words and, at one point, actually rises to the heard surface of the language:

FOOL. If a man's brains were in's heels, were't not in danger of kibes?

LEAR. Ay, boy.

FOOL. Then I prithee be merry. Thy wit shall not go slipshod.

LEAR. Ha, ha, ha.

FOOL. Shalt see thy other daughter will use thee kindly; for though she's as like this as a crab's like an apple, yet I can tell what I can tell.

LEAR. Why, what canst thou tell, my boy?

FOOL. She will taste as like this as a crab does to a crab. Thou canst tell why one's nose stands i' th' middle on's face?

LEAR. No.

FOOL. Why, to keep one's eyes of either side's nose, that what a man cannot smell out, he may spy into.

LEAR. I did her wrong.

FOOL. Canst tell how an oyster makes his shell?

LEAR. No.

FOOL. Nor I neither; but I can tell why a snail has a house.

LEAR. Why?

FOOL. Why, to put's head in; not to give it away to his daughters, and leave his horns without a case.

LEAR. I will forget my nature. So kind a father! Be my horses ready?

FOOL. Thy asses are gone about 'em. The reason why the seven stars are no moe than seven is a pretty reason.

LEAR. Because they are not eight.

FOOL. Yes indeed. Thou wouldst make a good fool.

LEAR. To take't again perforce! Monster ingratitude!

FOOL. If thou wert my fool, nuncle, I'd have thee beaten for being old before thy time.

LEAR. How's that?

FOOL. Thou shouldst not have been old till thou hadst been wise.

LEAR. O, let me not be mad, not mad, sweet heaven! Keep me in temper; I would not be mad!

(1.5.8-46)

I have already illustrated the other mode of Lear's experience and expression in this movement. But I must also include his last speech of the movement, for, aside from what it says, it reveals that sort of play writing of which Shakespeare was now a master—a way with another personality's words that requires that he feel below the surface of those words. The speech also shows us what is perhaps the beginning of Lear's realization that just as you cannot be rich in the possession of dirt, neither will language itself finally be capable of expressing one's greatest need. Were I preparing a production of this play, I would advise the leading actor to take a cue from this speech, and to realize that much of Lear's experience of himself is an expression of a metamorphosis from one sort of need to another, from a need for careless authority and others' flattery to a need for comforting as well as being comforted, for offering benediction instead of commanding it:

GONERIL.   Hear me, my lord.
   What need you five-and-twenty? ten? or five?
   To follow in a house where twice so many
   Have a command to tend you?
REGAN.   What need one?
LEAR.   O reason not the need! Our basest beggars
   Are in the poorest thing superfluous.
   Allow not nature more than nature needs,
   Man's life is cheap as beast's. Thou art a lady:
   If only to go warm were gorgeous,
   Why, nature needs not what thou gorgeous wear'st,
   Which scarcely keeps thee warm. But, for true need—
   You heavens, give me that patience, patience I need.
   You see me here, you gods, a poor old man,
   As full of grief as age, wretched in both.
   If it be you that stirs these daughters' hearts
   Against their father, fool me not so much
   To bear it tamely; touch me with noble anger,
   And let not women's weapons, water drops,
   Stain my man's cheeks. No, you unnatural hags!
   I will have such revenges on you both
   That all the world shall—I will do such things—
   What they are, yet I know not; but they shall be
   The terrors of the earth. You think I'll weep.
   No, I'll not weep.

Storm and tempest.

   I have full cause of weeping, but this heart
   Shall break into a hundred thousands flaws
   Or ere I'll weep. O Fool, I shall go mad!
                  (2.4.257-283)

The second movement of the play is by far the most difficult, technically, for the actor: vocally he must master techniques of breath control and phrasing not called for elsewhere in the text; for example, he must move from this—

> Tremble, thou wretch,
> That hast within thee undivulgèd crimes
> Unwhipped of justice. Hide thee, thou bloody hand,
> Thou perjured, and thou simular of virtue
> That art incestuous. Caitiff, to pieces shake,
> That under covert and convenient seeming
> Has practiced on man's life. Close pent-up guilts,
> Rive your concealing continents and cry
> These dreadful summoners grace. I am a man
> More sinned against than sinning.
>
> (3.2.51-60)

to this

> In, boy; go first. You houseless poverty—
> Nay, get thee in. I'll pray, and then I'll sleep.
>   *Exit* [FOOL]
> Poor naked wretches, wheresoe'er you are,
> That bide the pelting of this pitiless storm,
> How shall your houseless heads and unfed sides,
> Your looped and windowed raggedness, defend you
> From seasons such as these? O, I have ta'en
> Too little care of this! Take physic, pomp;
> Expose thyself to feel what wretches feel,
> That thou mayst shake the superflux to them,
> And show the heavens more just.
>
> (3.4.26-36)

The last of these speeches, to and about Edgar disguised as Tom o' Bedlam, is the first in a new mode of both experience and expression. Lear's need is being translated as he learns to feel, and this in turn touches his obsession with authority and its uses, with the abysses of nothing and everything that Professor Danson has discussed, and, as always, with needs of all kinds. He is beginning to struggle to see the human condition more clearly. These speeches are also good examples of the difficulty in casting this role adequately, for to encompass it is like learning, fully inhabiting, the late Beethoven piano sonatas. Once I had the honor to speak with the great pianist the late Clara Haskil. I had recently attempted, being brash and young, to play Lear, and admitted—quite correctly—that I had not even come close. "Ah yes," she said, "It is like the *Hammerklavier*, I suppose; when one's fingers can manage the notes, one hasn't lived through enough to understand it; and finally when one has suffered adequately and acquired something like wisdom, then—the fingers, alas, the fingers simply will not do what you tell them to do."

The third movement begins, as most third movements do in the major Shakespearean tragedies, with the hero offstage for about forty minutes. For the actor and character, I honestly believe this is a time that should be spent absorbing the experience just past. Not all the major heroes get the same amount of time (Othello gets only about twelve minutes), but I also think it possible that Shakespeare arranged the systems of intensities in these plays in such a way as to give his leading actor a rest before the final exertion; I assure you, one needs a breather. Hamlet is offstage for about forty-five minutes before returning to the graveyard, having learned that there is a divinity that shapes our ends, rough-hew them as we will. Macbeth gets about as much time as Lear, while Malcolm and Macduff test each other in England.

I will not elaborate the depths of the so-called Dover cliff scene—Professors Danson and McFarland have done that already, and eloquently—except to emphasize that I call it the so-called Dover cliff scene only because generations of critics have been so swept up in Shakespeare's and Edgar's topographical descriptions of heights and depths that they have forgotten that in fact the scene does not take place anywhere near the cliffs of Dover at all, and this, of course, is the object of Edgar's setting of the scene. It is into this episode that Shakespeare orchestrates one of the greatest entrances in this or any play. It is also a perfect example of how the rhythm of Gloucester's last words before the entrance actually effects the alteration of beat when the insane Lear steps into the acting place, and how the characters on stage already find a new reason to despair in the person of the old man who is now beyond it. These elements form the visual and verbal imagery of the beat simultaneously.

The spine of Lear's role, to use again the theater terminology, in the eighth exposure of him to us, collects in the new clarity of his insanity several strong threads of earlier concern. I have spoken often of the contrapuntal nature of the play; and this scene is almost a fugue, in both the musical and psychological senses of the word. Imagistically and rhythmically, Lear's concerns now are the definition of a man in terms of office, that is, the social function of authority; a sex nausea bred of the realization that the act of generation itself can be perverted; and finally a need within himself to comfort the two weeping men who listen to him, especially Gloucester. Again, the actor's techniques must utilize, in, as it were, each voice of this fugue, all the intensity and all the simplicity with which the actor has been charged previously.

It has often been observed that Lear's language itself changes in his ninth and tenth appearances on stage, but I think the astounding vividness of this change, both in the actor's feelings and in the audience's new view of his reality, needs to be reemphasized, refelt:

> Pray, do not mock me:
> I am a very foolish fond old man,
> Fourscore and upward, not an hour more nor less;
> And, to deal plainly,
> I fear I am not in my perfect mind.
> Methinks I should know you and know this man,
> Yet I am doubtful. . . .
> . . . .
> Do not laugh at me,
> For, as I am a man, I think this lady
> To be my child Cordelia.
>
> (4.7.59-70)

Compare:

Let it be so, thy truth then be thy dower!
For, by the sacred radiance of the sun,
The mysteries of Hecate and the night,
By all the operation of the orbs
From whom we do exist and cease to be,
Here I disclaim all my paternal care,
Propinquity and property of blood,
And as a stranger to my heart and me
Hold thee from this for ever.

(1.1.108-116)

John Gielgud has called Lear's speech to Cordelia in the fifth act (his tenth exposure to us) a graceful dance, a saraband. This is most perceptive. It also gives the modern actor a suggestive idea for adjusting the rhythm of the words themselves:

No, no, no, no! Come, let's away to prison:
We two alone will sing like birds i' th' cage:
When thou dost ask me blessing, I'll kneel down
And ask of thee forgiveness: so we'll live,
And pray, and sing, and tell old tales, and laugh
At gilded butterflies, and hear poor rogues
Talk of court news; and we'll talk with them too,
Who loses and who wins, who's in, who's out;
And take upon's the mystery of things,
As if we were God's spies: and we'll wear out,
In a walled prison, packs and sects of great ones
That ebb and flow by th' moon.

(5.3.8-19)

Professor Roche probed with valuable insight the last scene of Lear's life, the beat I have called a coda to the whole; but he deftly avoided much comment on Lear's "prison" speech, which I feel contains that "in-sight" any hero capable of tragic feeling must achieve. Indeed, I do not see how Tom, as one of the country's leading Spenserians, could have resisted pointing out the similarity of Lear's vision to that power which Nature has over her enemy in the Mutabilitie Cantos at the

181

end of *The Faerie Queene*—that power which both Spenser and Nature call "eterne in Mutabilitie," and which Chaucer, in a lovely lyric, called "stedfastnesse." The great difference is that Lear's terms are full, as Professor Goldman would point out, of specificity: Lear paints a realistic picture of court life, and one full at its best of gossip ("court news") and at its worst of corruption ("who's in, who's out"). He really does believe, as must the actor at this point, that it will be possible in Edmund's walled prison to tell old tales and exchange blessings, and that this communion in a mutual respect and love will "wear out . . . packs and sects of great ones / That ebb and flow by th' moon"—surely a reference to and a vision of that which is "eterne" in the midst of acknowledged "mutabilitie." That Lear is wrong, that anyone with a practical view of Edmund's needs would know that Lear's old man's dream is impossible, simply does not matter in terms of his emotional and moral achievement. I believe Lear's vision is in fact a deeply Christian one, but that does not matter either; in other words, the process of tragedy concerns itself as little with whether or not eventual salvation will be Lear's as with whether or not Othello is really going to be damned when Desdemona's face, pale as her smock, appears to him on the Day of Judgment. Whatever else tragedy, or Shakespearean tragedy, may be, among its most important criteria must be the hero's acceptance, first, that the action of the play just completed, or almost completed, has been his responsibility, and, second, though no less important, he must finally be able to define himself—in Laing's terms, his self in the midst of other selves. It does seem to me that the rhythms of Lear's emotions and needs across the expanse of this huge play do reach both of these rare innerly oriented achievements.

I have no easy answers for the questions posed by the last speeches in *Lear*'s coda, except to guess that Shakespeare himself needed to sum up all of his hero's qualities in a remarkably compressed episode, none of these in conflict with the accomplishment leading to and developed from his reunion with Cordelia. That tragedy states an achievement does not mean that it is not also—especially English Renaissance tragedy—inexpressibly sad. What answer after all can any feeling person give to Lear's question: "Why should a dog, a horse, a rat, have life, / And thou no breath at all?" Though there is bitterness and anger in Lear's question, he follows it with an equally great and sad realism. He is not mad now; he simply articulates the finality that any of us must accept when one whom we love dies: "Thou'lt come no more"—and then what must be the most incredible pentameter line in the English language, for only Shakespeare would have had the talent and the brazenness to write it—"Never, never, never, never, never." The images and sounds before us are not those of Doomsday, as Kent wonders; nor are they an artifact, an imitation, an "image of that horror," as Edgar murmurs. They are real, as real in pre-Christian Britain as they could be today; more important, they are real in the social phenomenon called drama, which, because of its own specificity and wonderment, heightens even an objective reality, and must leave both actors and spectators—at least at a good performance—numbed and, eventually, imaginatively and morally enriched.

Two final points remain. Several of my colleagues in this series of lectures have spoken about the so-called Stonehenge setting of this play, and it is true that I have seen productions (too many) that seemed actually to occur in the midst of those huge primeval rocks. That is taking the story's source in the annals of ancient Britain too literally. I liked Professor McFarland's observation on the open and nameless space *Lear* evokes. The fact is that *Lear* takes place primarily in space itself—not space as a cosmos, but space as a stage. If we envision the reality of this play as creating itself, moment by moment, beat by beat, phrase by phrase, in an absolutely open acting space, the reality of tempo, of image, and of idea will be heightened inevitably. There are two plays by Shakespeare that are most easily spoiled when an attempt is made by actors, designers, or directors to create a fairy-tale world, or a setting even remotely allegorical: they are *King Lear* and *The Tempest*. Both of these plays demand an acknowledgment of the stage as a magic and wild place which can be anywhere and everywhere, and which is contemporary and real precisely because the feelings projected from that place are specific and real. For example, the first big court scene in *Lear* will seem unreal and perhaps a little dull if we insist that its arrangement projects the old monarch, his good counselor, his two evil children, and his one good child, like two-dimensional playing cards. Certainly all these people are there, but they have reason—that is, the actors must have found motivation—to do and say what they do and say. Lear has planned this ceremony for a long time. He may be strong for his age, but he has a great deal of the wrong kind of self-esteem; and he wants this pageant of flattery to work. He has not imagined for a moment that it will not work; hence the scope of his fury at Cordelia. Having mentioned her, may I add to the long collection of remarks about her stubbornness, even, as Professor Roche called it, her feistiness, that she is real, too, and so are her needs and motivations: she is one of those people in the world (there are very few of them, but they exist) who simply, compulsively even, cannot lie.

Finally, it may be appropriate in a talk about *Lear* in the theater to observe that, while it is certainly a difficult play, it is, for actors of all the roles, a very generous one. It demands much intuitive and learned knowledge of style, of many styles, but these seem forever to metamorphose in new ways, each time one approaches the text for production. This is a quality for which actors who have done their homework are always grateful. I hope I do not offend anyone with this sort of analogy, but Shakespeare acted seems always to me much more akin to Mozart and Verdi than to such composers as Beethoven, Mahler, or Wagner. It is not a question of comparative greatness; rather, it is a matter of a style that breathes the flux of life itself with difficulties that are more fun to solve than others. There is, for example, more subtlety in the simple ¾ tempo in the lower strings that accompany the lyric love song on the violins in the first Prelude to *La Traviata* than there is in adjusting the phrasing of those famous first four notes of Beethoven's Fifth, or a difficult bassoon solo in a Mahler *Andante*. Here, as elsewhere, Verdi's simplicity is deceptive, as is, for another example, the apparently easy melodic line in the aria "Dove sono," in Mozart's *Figaro*. This is because such simplicity has been compressed from a density that, while complex, consists of great human perception—great enough to allow a variance from the norm, what German piano scores refer to occasionally as a "Luftpause," a millisecond's intake of breath that leaves a space in just the right place, and for which there is no possible printed notation.

I have called the texture of *King Lear* dense, too; but it is dense in the way the sextet from *Rigoletto* or the great ensembles of *Don Carlo* are dense: much is going on at once, but nothing is unclear, nothing is muddied. There is after all only one plot in *King Lear*, though for convenience we can speak, for example, of the Gloucester plot, or the Edmund plot, or the Edgar plot. But none of these is truly a subplot, and if any vocal and emotional line closely follows Lear's for emphasis, not contrast, it is that line of emotion written for Edgar, and not Gloucester. It is Edgar too who must become nothing before he becomes many others, each a helper in charity; and it is Edgar finally—I think it must be he, and not Albany—who bids no cannon shoot, who invites no one to a coronation, who tells nobody how he will regret reporting to the state the heavy deeds of the last scene. It is Edgar who finally articulates Lear's own great struggle: to speak not what is decorous, what one "ought to say," but, if one can, what one feels.

Library of Congress Cataloging in Publication Data

Main entry under title:

On King Lear.
  Contents: King Lear and the Shakespearean pageant of
history / Alvin B. Kernan—King Lear, acting and
feeling / Michael Goldman—Shakespeare, the King's com-
pany, and King Lear / G. E. Bentley—[etc.]
  1. Shakespeare, William, 1564-1616. King Lear—
Addresses, essays, lectures.   2. Lear, King—Legends—
History and criticism—Addresses, essays, lectures.
I. Danson, Lawrence.   II. Princeton University. Dept.
of English.
PR2819.O5   1981   822.3'3   81-47120
ISBN 0-691-06477-6   `   AACR2